Reboot

Reboot: How We Can Reprogram Our Internal Stories for Success

Copyright © 2020 by Paul Beauchemin

Hardcover ISBN: 978-1-7354305-0-8

Paperback ISBN: 978-1-7354305-1-5

eBook ISBN 978-1-7354305-2-2

Printed in the United States of America

Reboot

How We Can Reprogram
Our Internal Stories For Success

PAUL BEAUCHEMIN

To my dear wife Jinna who has been by my side for the last fifteen years in every step of our adventure.

To my four awesome children: Gabriel, Rene, Mireille and Laura.

To Norman and Jeannette—the best parents I could have ever had.

CONTENTS

Part IV: Operating System Bugs | 121

Part V: Unlocking the Code to Transformation | 155

GROUNDWORK

YOUR
SOFTWARE ARCHITECTURE

*"The great thing about a reboot is, that you can
learn from the past if you care enough."*

—Lexi Alexander

1

MY REBOOT

THE CONTRAST COULD not have been starker. I was sitting in a large living room with floor to ceiling windows on the thirtieth floor of a high-rise condo. There were ten other entrepreneurs in the room, all twenty to thirty years younger than me. We had all paid richly to attend a Master Mind event and sat there listening with rapt attention to Sam, a twenty-eight-year-old Kiwi who had immigrated to America only a year previously.

Standing in front of a magnificent view of the famous Chrysler Building in downtown Manhattan, Sam, dressed in a T-shirt and jeans, unshaven with voluminous, unkempt hair, did not appear to fit in.

I had met Sam a few years before. We were both enrolled in a course to learn how to build a subscription software business. Sam was a quiet, unassuming college dropout. I had come to know him through multiple phone conferences. He and I had been two of only three students who had built a successful and profitable software service.

Now, four years later, Sam had come to America as the owner

of a large international business. He was leading a firm focused on coaching people in how to be entrepreneurs. His income at that time had already climbed to eight figures a year.

I was old enough to be Sam's grandfather. Yet, here I was trying to glean a nugget of wisdom from him. When I met Sam, he was in debt and living in his parent's garage in New Zealand. Now he was the owner of the five million dollar condo in Manhattan we were all sitting in.

What he did to make that transformation was very simple, and on that day in NYC, it all clicked for me. Oddly it came while he was discussing quantum physics. Businessmen usually don't equate quantum physics to making profits.

After returning home, I recorded a seven-minute video to memorialize my insights. I conceived how to transform a George Orwell quote from bleak to enlightened. I will explain this in Chapter 9, Rebooting Your Memory Card, and clarify why this is so critical to "getting it."

Before the Master Mind event, I had felt trapped. After receiving a pink slip, I had been unfocused and aimless. Seven months later I had sold my home and was living a dream, traveling full time around the US and Canada in an RV.

That seven-minute video was the genesis of this book.

What did quantum physics have to do with my transformation?

And why was I even listening to a twenty-eight-year-old guru?

I am going to share that and much more. I am going to teach you to be free to choose whatever your heart desires.

2

HOW PROGRAM
SUBROUTINES
ARE TRIGGERED

Standing high on a bridge our protagonist is staring down on an ice-cold, raging river. His suit and tie are disheveled, his lip is bloody, and he is clutching some papers in his hand. He is drunk, depressed, and about to end it all.

The day had not gone as planned. The firm he owned was government regulated, and a year-end tax audit had uncovered large sums of money missing. He didn't face just bankruptcy and possibly jail, but most distressing, a scandal too.

His life had not gone as planned. He had never planned to stay in the crummy small town he grew up in and hated the firm he owned. He only operated it out of a sense of obligation to the memory of his deceased father.

When the auditor exposed the missing funds our protagonist rushed to find help. Only one man in town—a wealthy banker— had the resources to help him. But in this time of financial crisis, the old man scorned him and instead threatened to turn him into the police.

With all hope lost, our protagonist headed home to his large but decrepit home. His wife had done her best to rehab it. It was largely unfinished and the roof still leaked. When our protagonist arrived, he found his children screaming; one of them was ill. He had hidden the truth of his plight from his wife, so she did not understand his sudden strange behavior. When he repeatedly barked at all the kids, she screamed at him to stop torturing their children and to leave.

In anger, he overthrew a table and headed out to a bar. There he got drunk, and in a last desperate attempt to save himself, he sent a prayer to a God he had ignored most of his life. The answer to his prayer came moments later when another drunk at the bar punched him in the face.

Now here he was contemplating ending it all.

As our protagonist stood on the bridge he felt powerless and believed he was a failure at life. His life was not at all what he expected, and although not yet forty years old he saw no chance of turning it around. He clutched a copy of his life insurance policy. He believed his only real value was the dollar amount on those papers.

His internal monologue had been trained to feel triggered about something or someone for years. The repetition of triggers and anger and powerlessness built up to a climax. Our protagonist felt helpless to deal with his problems. In his mind, he was left with but one option. Life for all those around him would be better if he were dead.

⁓

Computers are programmed to think one way, just like our protagonist. To make computer software simpler, coders use small sets of instructions called subroutines. Subroutines perform frequently used operations within a software program. Think of a subroutine like a pattern that is easily accessed.

Our mental subroutines are also a set of instructions that are engaged whenever triggered. To get to the point of a major failure requires multiple glitches happening on in our life. Over time bad information piles up like garbage during a sanitation workers strike. In our computers, we have to reboot them to clear RAM memory of bad data. Likewise, we have to clean our memories of mental garbage before our brains "crash."

Our protagonist allowed himself to be ruled by one such subroutine that was the program of despair when the mind cannot find a way out of its problems. Will the man standing on the bridge ready to commit suicide go through with it? Will someone or something save him from his fate? At some point in our lives, we may have had thoughts of despair when there did not seem to be any way out. I know I have. Maybe you will come to such a point in the future as well.

In later chapters, I will reveal what happened to our protagonist and how you can transform your story to save you from your fate.

3

WHY YOU NEED TO LEARN TO CODE YOURSELF

_"If you always do what you've always done,
you'll always get what you've always got."_

—Henry Ford

WE ALL GET upset or angry or depressed occasionally. Life is full of happy times and sad times, and often it can be frustrating or boring and very often difficult to understand.

Crap happens in everyone's life—maybe even a lot of it. Sometimes a catastrophe happens— earthquakes, accidents, and disease—that is none of our making. Sometimes other people do bad things that make our suffering worse.

The question is, "What can we do about it?"

We can be perpetually angry.

We can accept it as fate and be apathetic, or worse . . . seek to end it all.

Or we can control one facet of our life.

When I was young and complained that someone got something more than I had received, my dad responded, "Tough! Life is unfair!"

Our perception is that life is unfair, and there is some injustice keeping us down.

This book is about what to do about that.

We all suffer throughout our lives. Getting sick and dying are of course the chief sources of misery. But we are also very much tormented by mental and emotional trauma.

I grew up as the first of eight children and hated my childhood.

Most of my childhood friends spent their youth playing sports or other games. My childhood was spent babysitting, doing laundry, cooking, and washing dishes. I changed more diapers by the age of twelve than most adults ever do.

Growing up my dad worked full time during the day and in the evenings commuted an hour to Boston to attend college courses. My mother often worked evenings cleaning offices in a nearby office complex.

As a result, I was often left alone in charge of my siblings. When my parents were home, my brothers and I spent a lot of time roughhousing. With only one sister (twelve years my junior), a "Lord of the Flies" atmosphere often prevailed. There was a constant struggle for leadership. To keep the house from burning down when my parents left, I was forced to maintain discipline. (That's not an exaggeration, by the way. The house did catch on fire once when the number two sibling was babysitting!)

I was small and skinny and lacked communication skills, so I shouted and fought in order to keep the household from falling into chaos. I was always afraid my siblings would gang up on me, so I ruled like a dictator. Not surprisingly, my siblings seemed to resent me for it. One brother even lit my bed on fire because I had withheld chocolate chip cookies from him!

When I did get time to "play" outside I worked a paper route. One of the more painful traumas I endured was when I'd pass the lady's house next door and she'd call out to me, "Hey homely." When a few of the young neighborhood girls started hurling that nickname at me, I would run home in tears. From then on I spent my free time retreating into books to escape their cruelty. I felt trapped.

By the time I was seventeen, I decided I had endured enough of the family and left home never to live permanently with my parents again. I resented my family and for the longest time felt cheated that I had to be a child-parent and couldn't enjoy my childhood. Although I tried to "divorce" my parents, they were key to two pivotal points later in my adult life.

Since my dad never made a lot of money, I knew I wanted something different. So I picked a major that guaranteed the most money on graduation. Even though I disliked chemistry and am not very good at it, I chose to major in chemical engineering. I chose a college that offered a work-study program because my parents were not in a financial position to pay for any of it.

Once again, life seemed so unfair. While my friends at college were out partying I was stuck studying calculus or thermodynamics. Besides the co-op job I held, I often worked second jobs while in college. For a time I worked the midnight shift at UPS and then would fall asleep in my morning classes.

After graduating I spent thirty-nine years working for the same chemical company. I only enjoyed the first two and last four years there. The rest of the time I was completely miserable in my job. I felt sick every Monday morning, trapped by obligations to my family and my debt. I went to work out of a sense of duty rather than any love for my job.

Later in life, I suffered infertility issues and a painful divorce. I've lost a sibling to suicide, broke my hip and shoulder, and suffered severe financial losses. My most painful traumas though were separations from my children.

Although your suffering is different from mine (and I am not looking for any pity), I'm sure that you have endured much too. I understand suffering. The reason I can empathize with your pain is a concept we will cover later—our ability to hurt others.

My suffering was amplified because I spent so much time resenting my problems. And although I didn't say it out loud, I was angry inside. Periodically I'd direct that anger at my parents, my ex-wife, my employer, and even God. But like many men, I mostly tried to keep my anger hidden.

✍

I recently read the book *LifeSpan* by David Sinclair, a Harvard PhD researcher investigating human aging. Sinclair seems certain that scientists are on the verge of extending human lifespans by several decades. It will become normal for people to routinely live to one hundred years old and beyond without suffering from debilitating diseases.

Extending health span (the time before death where we are fully healthy) will reduce or shorten much of the physical pain and suffering in the world. Many people though, like our protagonist, will still face mental and emotional suffering.

What you will discover in this book is that most of our mental and emotional suffering is self-created.

To me, Peter Drucker, a world-famous business consultant, seems to excellently sum up the challenge we have:

> *In a few hundred years, when the history of our time will be written from a long-term perspective, it is likely that the most important event historians will see is not technology, not the Internet, not e-commerce. It is an unprecedented change in the human condition.*
>
> *For the first time—literally—substantial and rapidly growing numbers of people have choices. For the first*

time, they will have to manage themselves. And society is totally unprepared for it.[1]

One of the leading trends in recent years is advocacy for physician-assisted suicide. One of the reasons for this is to eliminate suffering for people who have terminal illnesses.

A recent Canadian study of patients requesting physician-assisted suicide found that the main reasons were:

- Loss of control and independence
- Loss of ability to participate in enjoyable and meaningful activities
- Illness-related suffering (for example, pain or nausea)
- Fear of future suffering

Note that three of four reasons given were for mental and emotional issues, not physical pain. If 75 percent of our suffering is not physical, then increasing one's lifespan will not be the ultimate solution for happiness.

We have to learn to manage our mental and emotional states. The likely alternative is many of us will suffer decades of misery trapped in the slavery of hopelessness, fear, and anger. That will make our continuation on the planet too painful to endure. The trend of assisted suicide is really the manifestation of the failure to improve our stories in the face of extended lifespans.

People, when asked if they would like to live five hundred or one thousand years, usually respond in the negative. I would venture to guess that has something to do with perceived suffering. If I expected five hundred years of unmitigated fun and joy, it would be a no-brainer to want to continue to live. If I expected that most of those years would have lots of suffering, I would defer the opportunity.

---

1   https://www.azquotes.com/quote/570033

I've heard it said that man can endure unfathomable pain but cannot last without hope. When Drucker speaks of learning to manage ourselves, he is referring to our mental and emotional states. This is why you need to learn to re-code your mental programming. Henry Ford's counsel in the quote at the start of this chapter was as true in the 1920s as it is today.

People have been searching for a way to "learn to manage themselves" for centuries. This has spawned a huge industry of self-help books and experiential training. I've walked barefoot on burning hot coals a couple of times at self-help training events. Though exciting, the changes were always temporary. For most people, the goal of managing oneself seems unattainable.

Scott Adams, the creator of the comic strip *Dilbert*, has written several books on personal development. In *How To Fail At Almost Everything and Still Win Big* he writes that lasting change can only occur when you have a system in place. Hundreds of self-help books promote the importance of goal setting, but the number devoted to systems is far fewer.

We love reading aspirational information—it is part of our DNA. Inspiration releases lots of dopamine. However, inspiration is like a candle in the wind; easily quenched with the slightest breeze. The challenge with many self-help and motivational books is that they are very inspiring, but that inspiration lasts as long as a cool breeze. Crafting big dreams is rather fun and easy—like the cool breeze—but setting goals and creating systems require work and seem boring. But systems and goals appear to be mutually required to create success.

You're about to read about a system many very successful people use. I've used it myself and am certain it will help you manage yourself. This system is a method to help you understand what is causing you to act the way you do, and to give you the ability to control most of your own destiny. Parts of this system of thinking are found everywhere from ancient texts to the latest blog post. And now in this book, I will connect the dots for you.

Although you cannot control your destiny completely—there is a certain randomness to life—the strategies I offer you here will give you more of whatever you want in life while creating more happiness on your journey. These ideas and processes can help you to not feel powerless when things don't seem to go your way. Most importantly, you will learn that it's not about the journey, it's about the destination.

Here's a formula you can use to think about how this works:

Goals + System + Action = Results

Most people set goals. And some people have systems to help them achieve their goals. But taking action is one problem many people have with this formula. I will show you exactly how you can take action every time automatically.

Creating feedback by observing the results and making adjustments compounds the effect of the formula. This allows you to move into the top 20 percent or even 1 percent of any skill set or field you wish to conquer.

Today, many people who have been displaced from their jobs are told they should just learn to code, as though it's as simple as learning to take orders at a fast food restaurant. This advice implies that anyone can grasp computer programming language.

Computers are modeled on how the human brain works. Computers are programmed to perform certain functions. They are only as good as the quality of the information used to craft the program and the skill of the coder. I've taken that metaphor and developed a new way of looking at how we program ourselves and create results.

Think of your brain as the hardware in a computer. What is the operating system that controls that hardware? The operating system is the code that helps us to use our brain to get through life and is what I will address in the next chapter.

In this book, you will learn about how to modify your existing code as well as how to overwrite any old code with a new program. In fact, you have been using the brains' programming code all your life. All you need to get on a better path is to recognize what you have been doing and make some slight adjustments in your thought processes. I call it "debugging" your software. In other words, improving your skills at programming your brain will upgrade the information you use to create new paths.

The ideas on these pages will challenge many of the conventional beliefs that you have adopted. The suggestions may poke you in a place that is uncomfortable. When that happens you will encounter what I call a trigger. The "Debugging Software" in Chapter 14 is the technique you will use to evaluate a triggering event and then implement it to change your life.

This book will definitely require work. Work also triggers us. There is no "something for nothing" in the universe. Change won't come about just by reading words.

In this case, though, the work is to stop an activity, which is the opposite of how you probably think about effort. The activity you have to stop is telling yourself stories that are not true. Lying to or deceiving ourselves is one of the most pervasive operating bugs we have as humans.

Correctly interpreting the results of our actions means being honest with ourselves. If that makes you feel ill at ease, then it may be a sign that there is an opportunity for you to grow as a person. It is much easier to tell ourselves a story that is not true than to be honest.

Embrace the challenge and don't hide from it.

Whether you believe it or not, you will make an impact on the world, good or bad. You'll read why this is inevitable in Chapter 37.

What you will learn in this book:

- How to control emotions so your energy is not drained away.

- How to avoid procrastination and generate action to get the success you want.

- How to revisit old memories and come to peace with your past.

- How to shift the patterns your brain uses to keep you from seeing the truth.

- How to control your reaction to the onslaught of triggers you face every day.

- Fifteen new frames to transform your life with a new reality.

- A plan to make you the hero in your own life's story.

I will teach you how to identify your programming language and learn to modify the code that makes the computer of your mind work. This will allow you to live a happier, less stressful life and achieve the results you want. Like the protagonist in the story told at the beginning, you choose the story of your life. You too are the "protagonist" in your story.

PART I
THE
PROGRAMMING LANGUAGE

There was a boy whose family was very wealthy. One day his father took him on a trip to the country where he aimed to show his son how poor people live. So they arrived at a farm of a very poor family, for his son to observe. The father and son spent several days there. On their return, the father asked his son, "Did you like the trip?"

"Oh, it was great, Dad," the boy replied.

"Did you notice how poor people live?" asked the father.

"Yeah, I did," said the boy.

The father asked his son to tell in more detail about his impressions from their trip. "Well, we have only one dog, and they have four. In our garden, there is a pool, while they have a river that has no end. We've got expensive lanterns, but they have stars above their heads at night. We have the patio, and they have the whole horizon. We have only a small piece of land, while they have endless fields. We buy food, but they grow it. We have a high fence to protect our property, but they don't need it, as their friends protect their land."

The father was stunned. He could not say a word.

Then the boy added, "Thank you, Dad, for letting me see how poor we are."

4

NATURE, NURTURE, AND THE STORIES WE TELL OURSELVES

FOR A LONG time, there has been a debate about what influences our life the most: our genetics or our environment. Some people even suggest that our entire life is predetermined by our genetics and our upbringing, and there is little or nothing we can do about it. I suggest that another factor is more important than either of these, and we have total control over this third element.

A set of identical twins grew up in a dysfunctional household. The father was an alcoholic and very abusive to his wife and two boys. One son grew up to be an alcoholic like his dad. He couldn't stay in a relationship or hold a job. "How could I?" He mused. "I was destined to be a drunk! My dad was an alcoholic and so was his dad. It's my fate." He eventually became homeless and died of liver disease before he was fifty. Only a couple of people even bothered to attend his funeral.

The other son became a doctor and was kind and respected. The living hell he experienced growing up in his dysfunctional home disgusted him. He vowed early on that he would never be like his father. He never touched alcohol. He secretly attended church as a teen and later married a beautiful, kind woman. They raised a large family and were married for fifty years. He became the most respected man in his town. When he died, thousands attended his funeral to pay their respects.

What's the difference between the twins? They had the same genes and the same environment. The difference was the story they told themselves about their situation that determined what happened to them.

In the book, *The Switch* James Clement cites studies that show genetics controls less than 5 percent of our health. What if our environment accounts for an equal amount, another 5 percent? That means 90 percent of our health is controlled by our actions.

What if 90 percent of your life is not nature or nurture but is under your control?

And what if you control that 90 percent by the stories you tell yourself?

This is what the protagonist in our story is going to learn to do.

∾

Humans are natural storytellers. History was first passed down as stories. The Bible is a collection of meta-stories. We read books and go to movies because we crave stories. From little children to our eldest years, we are captivated by stories when all else fails to get our attention.

We tend to think of stories as coming from the outside, but in fact, our brain is constantly creating internal stories in order to make sense of the world.

Stories are the matrix of all human interaction—both internal and external.

Steve Jobs, the founder of Apple and Pixar, once pointed

out that the most powerful people in the world are storytellers. Apple's advertising under Jobs was as much story-based as the movies he made.

You are and have always been a fantastic storyteller.

You created the life story that you are now living. It may be an exciting story with lots of drama and chaos or a boring story with routine and structure. In either case, you are the one who made it all happen. And that point alone makes you powerful.

The point of the story about the twins is to point out the fallacy of the nature versus nurture dichotomy.

There is a third leg to the stool, and that leg, storytelling, is the most powerful of the three.

The way we see the world and ourselves is made up of thousands of stories we have been told, plus new stories we make up and then recite back to ourselves. We create and act out these stories in the theater of our minds.

If you want to be successful in whatever you endeavor to achieve, you have got to strip away your old stories—negative stories that prevent you from getting the results you want.

I intend to teach you that you have the free will and capacity to change and control your internal stories. And once you change your stories, your life will change.

This is because our stories control everything we feel and do.

This is not some secret kept from you by a hidden society. It's been exposed by thousands of people over the centuries. American novelist David Foster Wallace, in his famous talk *This Is Water*, says that like fish in water, we are swimming in a sea of stories. We cannot see them because stories are literally everywhere.

For most of history, the majority of humanity has been oppressed by the forces of nature or totalitarians. It is only recently—as the father of American management Peter Drucker observed—that large numbers of people have the freedom, as well as access to the know-how to change their lives.

When I was sitting in that Manhattan condo that January day looking at the New York City skyline and listening to Sam, I had a revelation. Sam was not in any way exceptional. As an immigrant with no connections, he had no network of "good ole boys" to help him. He was from a middle-class family in New Zealand that did not provide him with trust fund money or any seeming advantage. He was not charismatic, and everything about him was quite ordinary.

What I realized that day was that Sam had simply changed his stories about himself. He had started telling himself stories about what he was capable of achieving and had rejected the stories of his limitations. He had also told himself stories about how America was the land of opportunity where he could make a fortune. In four years' time, he had completely transformed his life. I realized then that it hadn't taken any superpowers or external intervention for Sam to do this. And I realized that I had made similar transitions many times in my life up to that point. Often it was to accomplish a large goal that I had thought previously impossible. The main difference between Sam and myself was that he had figured out how to create new stories consistently. And when he encountered a trigger, he was able to stick with the new story. He had buckled down to do the work of improving himself. In other words, Sam had crafted a system for himself to keep his stories focused on his goals. He minimized the time he spent in a failure loop when things went wrong.

As Scott Adams points out, you need a system of not just positive thinking or visualization, although both of these may help.

Here's the mechanism I came to realize that day in New York:

1. The stories we tell ourselves control our lives.
2. We create these stories from our memories.
3. Those memories are flawed and often based on childhood events that we encoded as victims.

4. We can change how we view our memories and thus change our stories.

࿇

Each of you reading this will have a unique reaction and craft your personal story around this information. That's because each of you has a unique history of stories and a set of biases. Some will pay more attention to some parts of the book and give a different meaning to other parts. Some will be triggered by this information and hide from it like an alcoholic hiding from reality.

It's quite amazing how unique we are. Even identical twins exposed to the same events can create distinctive stories just by what they pay attention to. One of the challenges of writing a self-help book is that prescriptions don't work. People are too different. Everyone is unique. Instead, this book is more of a framework for you to understand your mental construct.

One of the first things I did after returning home after that Master Mind event was to change my story about how I thought about my current situation. I had been forced to retire early after working at DuPont for nearly forty years. I had been telling myself I was a victim of their ageist policy. After the event, I changed my story and began viewing my retirement as a blessing. I was free to do something I had only dreamed of—spend my life traveling the country in an RV. I had no worries about getting up in time for work, fighting the snow. (I lived near Buffalo, New York.) No apprehension of two aspects of work I hated—dealing with dreaded performance reviews and project deadlines.

You may think it odd that it took me months to realize this, but there was one story that kept me stuck. What does that mean? Was there a plantation master keeping me enslaved?

࿇

One big story we all recite to ourselves that freezes us in place is that someone is coming to save us from our problems. We petition our parents, a spouse, the government, a charismatic leader, or even a godly savior for intervention. This storyline leaves us feeling powerless in the face of our problems and so we fail to take action.

This is the victim story.

In the face of helplessness, we tend to blame others or make excuses for our situation.

And as society grows more complex so does this culture of victimhood. It is a coping mechanism. It is much easier to blame someone else for your troubles than to figure out what to do when life is complicated.

Although you might not think of yourself as a victim, you still may behave in ways that expose a powerless internal story. Blaming others for our situation is one prime example of playing a victim. Making excuses is another.

Let's go back to our protagonist as we explore this victim story further.

5

STARTUP VIRUS CODE –
OUR VICTIM STORIES

"We understand everything in human life through stories."

—Jean-Paul Sartre

Our protagonist was not unlike many small children. He had been—as was common during the times in which he lived—hit and screamed at when young and had lost hearing in one ear.

Growing up he had dreams like many young children. He planned to go to college and travel the world. He thought he would become a famous architect. The small town in which he grew up stifled his imagination, and he despised his youth as he waited for a chance to escape. But over time circumstances changed. A war came, and he had to delay college. After the war, his father tragically died in his fifties. Out of a sense of obligation to support his mother and continue with the family business, he put his plans aside and took over the firm.

By his mid-twenties, our protagonist had given up on his dreams. Although he had moments of joy, he was a hollow man inside. He trekked through life a victim of the circumstances and his environment. His first twenty years had reinforced in him the belief of his powerlessness. He felt trapped just as I did.

You may have a completely different story than our protagonist. But no doubt, you learned there was much out of your control, and you were a victim as well.

Playing the victim is easy. It's our favorite story.

We all start our life self-centered. We live the "Me" story until we eventually toss it aside. Our experience in childhood teaches us how it works, and as we reach adulthood we have a choice about how much or how little of this lesson to embody.

The most important part of controlling our life is how we decide to confront these childhood phenomena when writing new stories. So much of being successful, however you define success, boils down to realizing that no one will save you and so you must not play a victim.

I had never thought of myself as a victim. If you had suggested I thought of myself as a victim, I would have resented your suggestion. I was independent and my own man!

But like most people, I tended to get angry when things didn't go my way. Not crazy angry, but angry enough to let out a curse or two. And then I would spend a few hours emotionally reliving the incidents, obsessively thinking about what I should have done or said. I blamed others when things went wrong or made excuses. Not every time, but enough so that often I wouldn't achieve my goals. For example, I often blamed my boss for my failure to achieve certain promotions. And in my first marriage, I blamed my ex-wife whenever we had a fight for not giving me the wedded marital bliss that I expected. And I blamed my employer for a forced retirement.

Although I would never have called myself a victim in any of these situations, subconsciously it was what I felt. I did not feel I had the power to change these situations or do anything about them.

When we experience a trigger, it's likely that some part of our psyche feels victimized.

We notice people who play out this victim story to the extreme. Those types publish manifestos of how they've been wronged and then go out and try to punish others with bloodshed.

But if you've ever heard someone say, "He made me do it" or "You make me angry" or "It's your fault," they are demonstrating their victim stories too.

Humans are born as completely helpless creatures who learn from their environment as they grow. To a baby, the world is absolute chaos. They lived in a nice, warm liquid for nine months, and suddenly they experience cold air and have to work to breathe!

The only part of that infant's brain that develops is the amygdala, the part that evaluates threats. Over the next few months and years that child experiences threats to itself: hunger, pain, uncertainty, and emotional trauma.

The truth is that every single adult has experienced events in their childhood that created chaos and fear in their minds. As children, we are victims of the people that raised us (usually parents) who had no clue how to raise children and were stuck on their own problems.

We were often victims of bullies who teased us for being "different." In a sense, we are victims of the cruelty of life itself. We all experienced the suffering of sickness and likely experienced the shock of learning of the death of someone close. At some point, we become aware that death is likely our fate as well.

In much of the animal kingdom newborns are on their feet in a few minutes and on their own shortly thereafter. Humans remain helpless for an extended period.

Children are vulnerable to both physical and emotional abuse. Our pre-frontal cortex (what you use to overcome the amygdala) is not completely developed until our twenties. As a result, when a child experiences oppression or even chaos their brain responds with fear due to their helplessness. Without the ability to reason, it is nearly impossible to fight back intellectually or emotionally.

Some children in emotionally abusive homes develop something similar to Stockholm syndrome. This is when a victim forms a bond with the person victimizing them. Often children will bring this bond with them into adulthood. Abused children may view their parents as infallible and justify all that their parents did. They learn to blame themselves for their mistakes or failures because their parents or caregivers told them it was their fault.

As people get older, they often turn the trauma of being victimized into a story of being a victim. Clever children learn at an early age that playing a victim can get them rewards. Maybe the reward is a treat or maybe it is "love" from one of their parents after being oppressed by the other.

Adults embody this knowledge and a significant number become professional victims. These skilled actors look to blame other people for their suffering and problems.

Why do we so often play the victim?

Psychologists talk about a payoff—a reward where we are "paid off" or in essence bribed—for our behavior. One payoff is that we receive love or sympathy when we can get others to perceive us as a victim.

Another payoff is getting attention for our behavior. We all want to feel important and that our life matters. Being perceived as a victim of some group is a payoff to get that feeling.

Sometimes people elicit a payoff in a manner akin to a mob boss extracting protection money. This is especially true in a family where a parent may withhold love in exchange for a certain behavior from a child. The payoff to the parent is the attention and "love" they get from the child.

Another strategy some people employ is hurting others in an attempt to make them feel more important. Being able to cause others pain gives them a feeling of power when otherwise they would feel powerless. And the hidden payoff for playing the victim is you don't have to take any personal responsibility for anything in your life. You can still be a helpless child depending on others to take care of you.

It's easier to offload pain and play the victim than to face your pain.

There are a couple of explanations about why people choose to play the victim so often. One explanation is that we have a predisposition for using less energy and doing less work. Our brains prioritize minimal use of energy as an evolutionary adaptation due to the frequent lack of sufficient food. By acting as a powerless being, the hope is others will take care of your problems, and you won't need to expend energy to solve them.

The other motive for playing the victim may be a response to the increasing chaos of the world. Three hundred years ago things changed very slowly. You could not play the victim and survive because society demanded self-responsibility. By the end of World War II, however, scientific advancements were doubling every twenty-five years, and by 2015 that pace had increased to a doubling every twelve months. In the face of this overwhelming fire hose flow of information, people need to find a safe space where they can retreat. Our brains work constantly to reduce complexity into simple patterns. When it is overwhelmed, the amygdala takes over. The amygdala controls our emotions and primarily the fear response. The more information we encounter, the more the world appears chaotic. And the unknown is frightening. "Staring into the abyss" is a common metaphor we use to describe this state as it perfectly depicts our fear.

Having curiosity about the unknown is a great strategy for dealing with the unrelenting growth of human knowledge. Fearing it or hiding from it is not. Government schooling is focused on memorization and passing tests rather than curiosity-driven learning. This has poisoned our natural inquisitiveness. We now need that trait the most to survive.

One hundred and fifty years ago the Darwinian effect of unaccountability would have culled many of today's professional victims. Today, we can play the victim and be quite irresponsible and still survive quite well. One way we observe this trend of people playing professional victims is on social media. People claim to be victimized by others who have no impact at all on their lives. People will tweet hatred at athletes, sports coaches or politicians who "harm" them. Yet the so-called harm is only something the athlete, coach or politician said or did that the tweeter disagrees with. A tweet can cause harm only in the sense that the person reading the tweet accepts it as impacting their life. The language of such users is often vile and angry beyond reasonable conversation.

We can't control the outcome of a sports game unless we're playing, so what is the payoff?

For Twitter users who express hatred, the payoff is the attention they get for the vile tweet and the feeling of importance they generate in their own minds. They feel superior in the same way a bully does when they hurt others. Anger expressed at another is projecting blame for our powerlessness.

When observing that behavior (not only on Twitter, but everywhere) you have to ask yourself, "Why are they seeking attention, and why are they so angry?" A person's obsessive use of Twitter in an abusive manner is likely a symptom of an addiction. There is likely an unresolved personal issue, which Twitter enables them to avoid facing.

Another way the victim script plays out in the public square is through identity politics. When we divide ourselves into tribes and view our tribe as victimized by other tribes, we identify as a victim. We feel powerless, which feeds our childhood victim scripts. Unscrupulous politicians and phony leaders use this feeling of weakness to paint themselves as "saviors." Note how a campaign spiel is often about protecting us from the "bad tribes."

This kind of identity politics creates an unhappy, angry populous seeking to hurt each other out of revenge and powerless to change. Cult leaders excel at exploiting this weakness in people.

In sum, the lessons about the victim stories are:

- We start life seeing ourselves as the center of the universe and interpret everything that happens around us as happening to us. Most people never grow out of this self-centered attitude.

- We were all victims in our childhood and sometimes victimized later in life. This is a reality of our existence.

- We transition from being a victim to playing the victim as we find this attitude or behavior pays off.

- Discerning when we are really victims versus just playing the victim is key to breaking out of failure patterns.

- If we cannot figure out mature ways to get love or attention, our subconscious resorts to playing out the victim story to get a payoff we crave.

- We sometimes seek to feel important by hurting others and "showing" them that they are inferior to us.

- Once our frontal cortex is fully formed, we can choose not to be so self-absorbed and not to use the victim story to get what we want in life.

- Victim stories are the source of 80 percent of our unhappiness. (Dissatisfaction stories account for the balance, as discussed in Chapter 31.)

- Unless we figure out how to stop this pattern in our system, our subroutine codes will keep us playing the victim. We will be unhappy, stuck in a pattern like an endless computer loop.

Think about what happened as you grew up. Cultural and technical trends encouraged you to blame others, make excuses, and feel victimized. Is it not surprising that so many of us have trouble taking responsibility for our stories?

The major challenge we have as adults learning to create the story we want is to not see everything as being about us. The less self-centered we are, the more control we have to overcome this tendency to play the victim.

Accepting the position that someone else is at fault for our situation keeps us from reaching our potential. I learned from my marriages that I cannot change other people. I can only change myself. Playing the victim, blaming others, and making excuses never moved me toward my goal of a happy marriage, a successful career, or deep friendships. Playing the victim always moved me further away from whatever I wanted—especially if that was peace of mind and joy.

That day when I was sitting in Sam's condo I had felt trapped. I had worked for DuPont for nearly forty years, and when a merger between DuPont and Dow Chemical occurred, I was told to retire. I hadn't made any plans to retire yet and though I lived in a beautiful house on a lake, I still had a mortgage, rental houses, and recurring bills to pay. I believed I had to keep working.

I had been searching for and starting business ventures for twenty years at that point. I had started an Amway business, invested in many rental houses, founded a software service for private investigators, and was running a digital marketing service. So Sam's message struck a nerve with me. I thought his message would give me the key to what I was searching for.

I felt that if I found the right business it would "save" me from my circumstances. And Sam was the most recent version of the perfect guru to help me out.

Feeling trapped, being powerless to change, is another type of victimhood. I was more than happy to blame my old boss for my financial circumstances. I was great at making excuses for why I wasn't making as much income as Sam. I was angry with Father Time, as I believed that somehow my age was hindering my success.

You are not stuck. No one is. Feeling trapped is just a story—a victim story.

I feel sad for young people who feel trapped and think life is hopeless and that their circumstances won't change. Life seems the same day after day, but over time nothing stays the same. In reality, everything changes. People who are older can look back at their lives and see that their stories changed, often dramatically, from one phase of their life to another. The story we had as a child was much different from our teen story and subsequently was different from our young adult story. As our circumstances, depth of knowledge and experience, and level of emotional maturity changes, so do our stories. Change seems to take place slowly, primarily because we cling to the past. Yet change can also happen rapidly. In fact, sometimes change happens in fractions of a second. The change I experienced at Sam's condo happened in a microsecond, yet was years in the making filled with bad stories.

Assuming responsibility for your life takes courage, but the rewards are immeasurable. Feeling powerful instead of powerless gives you a sense of self-worth that is worth it. It also takes incredible courage to invalidate our victim stories since we have organized our entire life around them. In Chapter 14 I am going to introduce you to the Debugging Software where you will learn to examine why you are telling yourself victim stories and discover tools to create a new story.

When we were young and our minds were most receptive to new knowledge, misguided educators promoted the idea of teaching self-esteem. Simultaneously, they preached to students the contradictory idea that they are victims. Self-esteem comes from growing in competence and responsibility. It does not come from receiving participation awards or thinking of ourselves as victims.

Everyone has a choice to play the victim or be responsible for themselves. And you can make this choice in less than a second.

The famous Canadian psychology professor Jordan Peterson gave a magnificent explanation of the topic of oppression and being a victim in one of his university lectures. Peterson is a You-Tube superstar and author of *Twelve Rules For Life.* Ten minutes of his talk have been posted on YouTube titled "Jordan Peterson – His Finest Moment" that is worth your time to understand this at a deeper level.[2]

The antidote to playing the victim is taking personal responsibility for your life.

That statement triggers some people so much that they protest to ban speakers at colleges who dare to speak about it[3]. People don't want to hear that their life's problems are of their own making. The idea often evokes deep reflexive anger because the alternative is to accept their failure as their own fault, and leaves them with no one to blame.

You can choose to accept or reject this premise. Those that reject it spend their whole life hoping someone will save them. They will be deeply unhappy.

No one is going to save you! Stop playing the victim.

---

2   "Jordan Peterson - His Finest Moment," https://www.youtube.com/watch?v=-XvI6Y5Yq8o&t=303s

3   For example, Ben Shapiro has routinely been forced to cancel talks at many colleges due to riotous behavior by students

6

THE PATH OUT OF
CODE FLAWS

WE ARE BORN alone, we die alone, and all our memories are ours alone. Though people may be near you, no one can feel your pain; no one has your thoughts or memories. No one can ever totally understand you. This is an existential truth. Failing to face this reality hampers our growth and tempts us into all kinds of self-delusions. Looking outside ourselves for a solution to our problems is a shell game.

Paradoxically our biggest fear is being alone. We often avoid being alone at all costs. We spend years searching for a lifelong partner, a "soul mate" who can "complete" us. This usually leads to unrealistic expectations when we form a union. We can search the world for the perfect companion we all desire, but unfortunately, no one can make us whole. Some people who can't find a human companion will adopt an animal as a pet to avoid being alone. These opposing impulses are part of the duality of nature.

When we are alone we have to face the person most responsible for our lives—us! Only the person looking back in the mirror can save us.

Because we are singular creatures, much of the pain and suffering we endure is self-inflicted. We torture ourselves with thoughts of inadequacy or helplessness or revenge.

When we claim that we are victims, we become powerless to change. I cannot save you from all your pain and suffering. If you do not want to take control of your life, the rest of this book will be meaningless.

So, how do we save ourselves?

First, we must understand that intrinsically we are creators. Humans are pretty good at destruction as well, but basically, we are better at turning chaos into order.

We are actually pretty happy when we are creating. We love to build things, draw pictures, write, cook, sew, and all kinds of other creative activities. The reason we love these activities is that creation is a very goal-oriented process that we will discuss in Chapter 7.

We often think of those who engage in a specific artistic occupation as being creative. But really everyone is gifted at a very fundamental level. Everyone creates the stories that dictate their life. You are the writer, director and lead actor or actress in your life's story.

We are powerful because we create our stories. Just like programmers writing code or playwrights developing a script, we are in control of what results our stories produce. You can make the protagonist in your story (you) a hero or a villain.

Conversely, choosing to destroy (that is, engaging in destructive behavior), while it may feel powerful, always ends up in unhappiness. Destructive behavior is a sure sign that we are playing a victim and acting powerless. Destroying or hurting others gives a false sense of power that ricochets back at us.

The premise of this book is that you, wittingly or not, are

creating the story of your life. People who succeed in getting what they want out of life create their stories with careful consideration and confidence. They reinforce behaviors that work and forget about failures quickly.

People who are stuck have little confidence that their story will get them what they want. They get frustrated and despondent when they reinforce their mistakes. These types of people often look to become part of someone else's story rather than creating their own. When you are part of another's story, you lose control of your destiny. Throughout this book, you will learn strategies to create different stories than the ones in which you may be stuck.

You will find that you are indeed quite powerful and do not have to live a life like Walter Mitty. Mitty is a meek, mild-mannered fictional character in a James Thurber short story "The Secret Life of Walter Mitty." Although he fantasizes about being a hero, he lives out his life in a state of fear and inaction. In my youth, I was the perfect Walter Mitty. To escape bullying I read books and daydreamed about my perfect life someday.

The life you have right now is at least 90 percent your own creation. Sure, random events and genetics play some minor role. But not enough for you to lie back and give in to fate.

How much you get out of this book will depend on to what degree you accept this reality and to what extent you want to claim you are a victim.

Here are the important points to remember:

1. You are a creator.
2. Being a creator gives you power.
3. The power you have is over:

    a. What you chose to remember and
    b. What you give meaning to when you remember anything.

4. When you accept this power, you will no longer feel like a victim, no matter the circumstances, and you will have complete peace of mind.

There is hope in finding purpose in life. We just have to get past the basics.

7

A REASON TO MODIFY
OUR CODE – PURPOSE
DIRECTED LIVING

IN PSYCHOLOGY COURSES, one of the first concepts taught is
Maslow's hierarchy of needs. Maslow conjectured that resolving
the basic needs first drives human action.

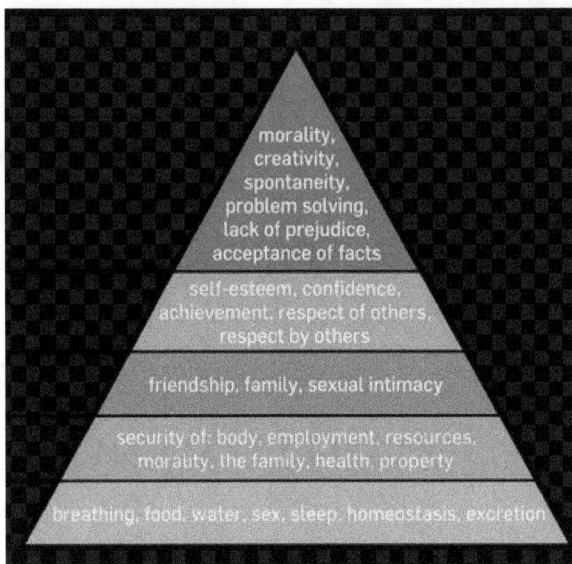

Once our basic needs are met, then we climb the pyramid seeking security, then friendship and family until we fulfill all our needs. Eventually, we may seek out a greater purpose to give our life meaning.

This pyramid is a continuum, which we move up and down throughout our lives. Our various life experiences are not at the same level. For example, a person may be very confident in their work or business and quite wealthy. But they have no confidence in dealing with sexual intimacy or are even in poor health. This is illustrated by the Japanese billionaire who booked a trip to the moon and announced he was looking for a female partner to take with him. There are better ways to find a wife!

Understanding Maslow's pyramid can also help us understand other people. We may live in a tribe where most of our needs are met, and we are looking for a higher purpose. We may not understand why people in another tribe may not have the same priorities as us. The environment is one such example. If a person doesn't have enough food or water, worrying about how much plastic is in the ocean is not going to be a priority. Creating a YouTube sermon condemning capitalism in first world countries won't make a difference. Helping those people who don't care about the environment to move up Maslow's hierarchy is what will produce the results we want.

People need goals and often are somewhere along Maslow's hierarchy seeking a goal. Early in life, we seem oriented to setting and achieving goals. We focus on graduating from high school or college; getting a job; getting married; buying our first car or house; having a child.

The bigger the goal or purpose, the more exhilarating our life journey is and the more personal growth is required to achieve that goal. Even engaging in hobbies we enjoy can give meaning to our everyday life or at least provide opportunities for mindfulness.[4]

Our brains seem to have evolved to be driven to seek goals. Our operating system rewards this goal seeking with dopamine making us temporarily happy. When we tell ourselves that our life is boring, we often seek thrills to get this dopamine kick.

When we become aware that we are going to die, what keeps us motivated to survive? Continuously initiating the thrill of that dopamine high may be all that keeps us going.

When we don't have a goal, we create hopeless stories of failure. Psychologists call this depression. Without a purpose, we convince ourselves that life is pointless and give up. Many people who get stuck in this storyline turn into nihilists—that is, they see life as meaningless. A more apt name for depression might be "dopamine deprivation."

Having goals and working toward them gives meaning to what

---

4   Mindfulness is like meditation in that it diverts your mind from its endless self-absorption – to be discussed in Chapter 27.

we do and how we react to life on a day-to-day basis. It enables this creation impulse within us and rewards us with dopamine.

When we stop setting goals for ourselves, our minds often lead us to seek out that dopamine hit from somewhere else. We might get a buzz from having an affair, embezzling money, or jumping out of an airplane. We tend to gravitate towards high-risk behavior, thinking it will give us a bigger high.

It's important to understand that we are biologically driven to be goal-oriented. And if we have achieved all of the lower goals on Maslow's hierarchy, then we need to find a greater purpose. Without it, we are tempted to engage in behavior that we may regret. I will discuss this concept further in Part VI.

Here's where goal-seeking behavior becomes interesting.

To achieve a goal or purpose requires us to change. The further the goal is from our current state, the more personal change is required. Personal growth is the accelerator pedal that makes achieving our goals go easier and faster. The more we grow the bigger the goal we can achieve, and the more "luck" we encounter.

Growth appears to be integral to our evolution. We observe in nature that organisms are healthiest when they are growing and expanding. Our biology rewards growth chemically. Growing produces good results; lack of growth produces decay.

In other words, humans are healthiest when they are fulfilling a purpose for their existence. In fact, the grander the purpose, the happier we will be working toward that purpose. There is a universal desire to make ourselves the hero of an epic journey that places us at the summit of Maslow's pyramid. I'll discuss this more in Part VII.

Once organisms stop growing, they start to die. Likewise, when humans stop growing, we start to decline toward death. We start to engage in risky behaviors, eat poorly, and lose hope. We give in to "fate," and start telling ourselves that we are the victim of the universe and powerless to change any of our circumstances.

What impairs our growth the most? Seeing ourselves as victims and blaming and hurting others. In an effort to find "justice" for their own situation, people who have stopped growing become destroyers and try to inflict the maximum pain onto others. They believe they can raise themselves up by pushing others lower. It's time to understand what makes us tick.

8

UNDERSTANDING OUR SYSTEM HARDWARE

"Remember particularly that you cannot be a judge of anyone. For no one can judge a criminal until he recognizes that he is just such a criminal as the man standing before him, and that he perhaps is more than all men to blame for that crime."

—*The Brothers Karamazov*
by Fyodor Dostoevsky

BEFORE ANY CODER can begin work they have to understand the capabilities of the hardware on which they are programming. When I bought my first computer, a Radio Shack TRS-80, it had 4 KB of memory and could handle only a few lines of BASIC programming language. Today my iPhone XS has 256 GB of memory, yet it still has limitations.

Like those two computers, as we as humans acquire more knowledge and capabilities, we find there is still so much more to explore and learn, requiring new processing competence. Part of the challenge is that we usually think we understand ourselves. We believe it is difficult to change ourselves. We get stuck thinking that we have the old TRS-80 processor with 4 KB of memory. We look at other people and think they have more advanced hardware and thus are more capable than us.

Our systems, or brains, have evolved over hundreds of thousands of years. For most of those millennia, life was "nasty, brutish and short," as Thomas Hobbes noted. The basic needs of food, shelter, and procreation drove our actions. There was no time to worry about the environment, other people's feelings, or what others thought of us. The development of the frontal cortex came later in the evolution story. Our amygdala developed first to help us survive the threats in the world and still dominates our actions, which has led to lots of tribalism and violence in the world. Historically, we are very irrational creatures regulated by our amygdala trying any way we can to survive. In the last few decades, we have started to use our frontal cortex to try to scale back some of the survival code deeply embedded in our DNA. But mostly we use it to justify our irrational actions.[5]

With that in mind, let's look at two competing fields of thought about human behavior: one that assumes with the right "rules" you can fix human behavior and the other that accepts and works within the limitations of human flaws. Let's examine them and determine what our system hardware is capable of.

An Englishman (and Catholic Saint), Sir Thomas More, wrote the book *Utopia* in the sixteenth century. A utopia is a perfect society where there are no wars and people live in perfect harmony with each other and nature. Karl Marx seized on More's work and promoted it in his manifesto. The utopian view is that you can engineer social systems to change the behavior of society. The "highly evolved" people will decide what that standard is. The

---

5   A good read is *Predictably Irrational* by DanAriely

utopian view is that self-interest is greed and needs to be eliminated. But self-interest is so deeply embedded into our DNA it is more probable to eliminate fear.

Countries like the Soviet Union, China, Cambodia, Cuba and Venezuela have tried to implement that perfect society with disastrous results. Hundreds of millions of people were murdered and many more suffered from policies aimed at creating the perfect society. However, the idea is so appealing it continues to have a following today, especially among idealistic youth.

Despite the failures of this type of society, the argument is that with the right people in charge, it would work. It's an appealing idea.

My wife grew up in communist China in the late 1960s. During the Cultural Revolution, the government forced people to get rid of the kitchens in their homes and use a community kitchen. Everyone got the same amount of food no matter the effort put into reaping the crops. Soon people figured out that they didn't have to work very hard in order to be fed. However, once a sufficient number of people stopped working, food output dropped dramatically. In the end somewhere north of 60 million people starved to death.

The macro results of this ideology speak for themselves, but this type of philosophy also can infiltrate into our personal stories. Let's examine this utopian philosophy and the impact on your story.

Recently we find people fighting for "social justice" and find that people promoting this idea of social justice:

1. Tend to feel oppressed (victims),
2. Blame others in order to elevate themselves and lower their oppressors, and
3. Excuse their role in creating their current circumstances.

This type of thinking is counterproductive to good goal-seeking behavior.

It stunts personal growth. Whenever you fail to take personal responsibility and put your hope in someone else changing, you lose all your power. Growth requires energy or power.

A social justice warrior may think they have power when they demand other people to change. Yet doing so depends on others to change. And you can't force people to change their minds. China's Chairman Mao said, "Political power comes from the barrel of a gun." He and many like him waged a war with the populace to eradicate bad thinking. They found the only way to abolish bad thinking was to kill the bad thinker. This approach leads to lots of deaths, and if you're not a dictator, it results in exhaustion, disillusion, and nihilism.

The utopian paradise storyline creates undesirable results both at the personal level and society level. It is in conflict with human nature and behavior patterns. Our hardware is not capable of running this operating system—no matter how appealing.

A second viewpoint is one that many Christians promote: humans are flawed beings and cannot change without some external redemption.

Russian writer Fyodor Dostoevsky explains the concept of original sin well in his novels *Crime and Punishment* and *The Brothers Karamazov*. Each book includes layers of wisdom buried throughout. Two main themes stand out. The first is that we are the only species that consciously knows what causes us pain. We then knowingly and willfully inflict pain (both mental and physical) on others and ourselves. His second point is that we are all complicit in causing the suffering of others. (It may be that some primates hurt other members of their tribe, but these actions are taken to assert dominance. Animals don't blame others for their pain. There are no Josef Mengele's in the primate world.[6])

This awareness that we inflict pain on others is a dark side of our being that we try to hide from others. American psychiatrist M. Scott Peck best known for his book *The Road Less Traveled,* also wrote a book called *People of the Lie* in which he points out that people would rather lie to themselves and attack others than face their own failures. Peck calls this the root of evil behavior. Animals are not aware of their lies, so this dark impulse is a uniquely human capability.

Every human engages in the behavior of hiding their failures with outward attacks on others. We all also hide this to a great degree and think of it as our "dark" side. Oddly, the people who don't try to hide their dark side we call insane! Some hide it better than others, and some pretend they have evolved beyond this. Don't believe them! Their hubris causes harm to others. Perhaps this knowledge of our ability to hurt others is really original sin (the knowledge of good and evil as the Bible teaches).

When we harm others we are basically blaming someone else for our problems or playing the victim. We cannot grow when we *play* the victim (as opposed to *being* a victim). I've deliberately used the word *play* whenever I refer to this behavior. We are acting a part in a story that we scripted and directed.

Children are often victims of abuse at the hands of adults. However, they learn quite early in life how to play the victim to get what they want. Many, if not most of us, carry these lessons throughout our adult life.

Harming others is also unhealthy for the abuser and keeps them from growing. Seeking to gain through the suffering of another creates internal conflict and amplifies one's own suffering.

---

6   · The "Angel of Death" Mengele performed deadly experiments on Jews in German concentration camps

I am sure that there is a "Me" story that is driving the desire to harm others. Me stories are those secret stories we have that are all about us. (See Chapter 14 for more discussion about Me stories.) Resolving Me stories is essential to our growth.

Achieving our purpose requires us to find ways for personal growth and expansion of who we are. At the same time, we should focus on reducing the harm we do to others. In other words, not projecting our internal frustration as someone else's fault.

There are many paths to achieving personal growth. The path we choose is just that, a path. It ceases to be a good path when we find that we can no longer grow doing what we are doing—in other words, when we get stuck in a repeating pattern of behaviors and results. Oddly, our brain sees this repetition as order even if we are stuck.

Some people will switch environments, jobs, or partners and repeat the same patterns to maintain brain order. This is not changing our path, but it is a pivot point and opportunity for change. For more insight into how to grow and for a discussion on pivot points see Chapter 46.

There are two major reasons why people inflict pain on others. Like the primates, we may seek to assert our dominance. The drive to have the upper hand in our relationships is deeply embedded in our consciousness. When we see someone or some entity that we view as more powerful, we "mind read" their behavior. Our fears lead us to assume they want to dominate us and hence hurt us. This gives rise to conspiracy theories about Big Pharm creating poisonous vaccines or the Military-Industrial Complex manufacturing wars to keep killing people.

As society climbs Maslow's pyramid this type of conduct is becoming increasingly less acceptable. Most people agree that harming others in the pursuit of dominance is no longer tolerable in today's culture. But there is a more subtle reason we harm others. That behavior comes about when we choose to play the victim.

Our desire to hurt others begins with our own suffering. To find a reason for that suffering we tell ourselves a story (based on bad memories) of some harm that we believe others inflicted on us. We convince ourselves that our story of others harming us is the cause of our suffering. This deludes us into thinking that we are justified in seeking some retribution for the alleged cruelty.

We are not entitled to hurt others because we are in pain. Hurting others will never satisfy us or help us to grow. In fact, the pain inflicted on others boomerangs back on us in some karmic way.

Our amygdala (the most ancient part of our brain, sometimes called our reptile brain) is programmed to have four reactions to threats:

- Fight
- Flight
- Freeze
- Fawn

These reactions all take place without conscious thought.

Reacting to threats with a physical or verbal assault is the fight response.

Running away from the danger is the flight response. Unless a tiger is attacking us, most threats today are not deadly, and we need to face them directly. Running from them is acting powerless. Blaming or making excuses or running from our own personal responsibility to grow and become better is the freeze response. It is playing the victim. Subverting our own story to someone else's is often stated as a "go along to get along" strategy. It is the fawning response when people convince themselves that "keeping the peace" is more important than facing the threat. In truth, this is just a way to act powerless.

Our brain sees the world in terms of threats to our survival. So, unless we are well trained, we will react to many events as a threat and seek to turn around and hurt the one who we perceive is threatening us.

The other part of Dostoevsky's theme is that we are all responsible for all the evil we see in the world. This is a very hard message to accept. It's easy to see the other tribe as being responsible for the problems in the world and believe our tribe is good.

Social justice warriors raise awareness that certain behaviors have caused pain. To that extent, they have a valid message. As I note in my Debugging Software script, it is valuable to see the other person's point of view.

Before we debug our script, there is a strong urge to label those who disagree with us as evil and act self-righteously. What if we are all intimately connected, and accusing others of being evil is just a projection of our inner self?

In Chapter 37 I discuss how we are connected, and why it's important to understand that connection. Swiss psychologist Carl Jung identified this as a collective unconscious, which links everyone's subconscious thoughts.

If we observe how humans have interacted over time, we can see how collectively we have changed how we treat each other. For example, for much of history enslaving other tribes was the normal behavior among all humans. It is only in the last two hundred years that we started treating this behavior as inappropriate.

Now some people may think that they are more evolved than others and look down at those whom they view as less evolved. This very act of viewing others as below you actually dehumanize them and contributes to the evil in the world. In Chapter 28 I discuss how judging others harms our own personal growth.

Every person is constantly sowing seeds of themselves wherever they go and whatever they do. Focusing on others as the problem fails to correct that. All seeds contribute to the universal human condition and community, and we all have the responsibility to put down good seeds

Our system hardware seems to have two opposing constraints. First, there is the self-interest directive, which pushes us apart from each other. Second, is the network connectedness, which links us in shared responsibility for the results in the world.

There is a duality in the world that appears everywhere once you become aware of it. You will see it appear several times throughout this book. Two opposites always seem in conflict. Our default position is to pick one side and defend it with all our power. You will discover that there are no sides. Fighting for your side because it's "right" is akin to cutting off your right hand because the left hand claims it sins.

This intramural fight is going on very publicly in US politics. Each side is dug in and expects the other to compromise to their viewpoints. Only acknowledging the reality of both aspects can any resolution come to pass.

9

REBOOTING YOUR MEMORY CARD

"Those who control the present, control the past and those who control the past control the future."

—George Orwell

WHAT WE SEE in the world is nothing but our memories.

Most of us are certain that our memories are the absolute truth about what happened. Therefore, if we hate the way the world looks, it is a reflection of how our mind is making sense of it based off our memories.

Our mind uses memories to categorize the past and filter out what we disagree with. We only remember and give meaning to what we pay attention to.

Our certainty about our memories and negative aspects of life we experience create endless loops in the operating systems that are our brains. These loops repeat the same patterns over and over. Sometimes our computer RAM (random access memory—the easily accessed memory) becomes so corrupted that we have to reboot our computer to make it run better. Likewise, cleaning your memory card is the key to allowing you to reprogram your life story.

Are you living in the past? If you are reacting to memories or hurting others based on something they did in the past (even if it was five minutes ago), then you are living in the past. Most humans are living in the past (feeling guilt) or worrying about the future (feeling anxiety) but not living in the present (feeling joy).

It was during Sam's discussion of quantum physics that I had my aha moment. While I was returning home from Sam's Master Mind event in New York City, I was trying to formulate how this insight would work in real life. I thought about what George Orwell said, "*Those who control the present, control the past and those who control the past control the future.*"

When I first read this Orwell quote, it appeared to imply dark malfeasance from tyrannical governments seeking to control us.

Maybe that was Orwell's intent, maybe not. No one was or is able to read his mind (although we all love to engage in mind reading). But, if flipped around, I thought, maybe we can change our interpretation of this quote in a way that can free us from our past so we can control the future.

Before we can create and control our stories we need to understand how our brain forms a memory. Memories are how we interpreted events in the past based on our beliefs and values at the time they were formed. Memories are not some absolute truth.

We live in the now. Let's call it the quantum moment. Life happens instantaneously and then our brain dumps knowledge of events into our memory bank. Every moment we experience becomes the past and it ceases to exist in the present reality faster than we become aware of it. The past is therefore just a memory. It doesn't exist. Even if there is a photo or video of a past event, it is only the meaning we assign to that event that gives the event any significance. The future is what we are creating every moment with our stories.

The problem is that the future we want to create is often dragged down by the past we keep referring to. We weave our past memories into a rope tied to an anchor keeping us from moving forward.

As a result, when we seek to reach our goals a fog of fear obscures the pathway. Clearing that path requires that we understand the stories driving our behavior. And we must understand the results from our actions.

Most of us are certain that our memories truly represent what happened. But memories are not the truth! Two people can experience the exact same event and have very different memories of what happened. You'll know this to be true if you are a witness to an auto accident and compare your account to others at the scene. One person will remember the event one way, while another will remember the event in a completely different way.

The memories you create are based on the meaning you assigned to the event. The meaning that you attach to any given event is biased by your beliefs, values, and tribal influences. Many of the memories formed in early childhood shape every new story you create.

When I was young our history textbooks depicted the American Founding Fathers as wise heroes. Their sacrifice created the greatest nation on earth. Today's textbooks depict the Founders as ruthless slaveholders who oppressed the native people.

Which memory is the truth?

It depends on what we pay attention to and what meaning we assign to each event.

The key concept to understand is not that the past events did not occur. They may or may not have occurred (we misremember, forget or make stuff up all the time). The important thing is to understand how we interpret events. First, we decide which parts of the event we want to pay attention to. Then we can attach a specific importance, value and meaning to the event based on our unique beliefs, experiences and indoctrination.

In other words, the story of your life is written, directed, and acted out by you. And how you play it out in the theater of your mind clouds how you see every new event that occurs.

We can view memories of past events like a Rubik's cube. Look at the event from one angle, and we will see one aspect. Change our viewpoint, and we can see something completely different. Like the twin brothers in Chapter 4, we have the choice about what meaning to assign to those events and that is the key to our life.

Here's the sequence to think about:

1. We draw our stories from our memories.
2. We decide what meaning to give to past events and what events to pay attention to.
3. We are not stuck with giving past events the same meaning that we did yesterday or last year.
4. When we control what we think about the past events we recall, we control our future. The past is no longer anchoring us down.

I rewrote my memory of George Orwell's famous quote to transform it from a dark, foreboding intimation to make it a positive message:

"We can control the present by deciding how we remember the past. Therefore, we are in complete control of the future."

Orwell's quote implied that external forces are controlling us. The truth is that only our choices have any real control. And the most important choice we can make in life is how we look at our memories. I've re-written most of my memories from the past. I now see my parents as heroic figures in their efforts to raise eight children on a small income. I remember my dad practicing a speech in front of the family for a public speaking course he was taking. At the time, I thought nothing of the tremble in his voice and shaking hands as he held the paper. Now I see how much fear he had to overcome to reach his goal of getting a college degree.

I can see how my upbringing forced me to grow far beyond just an ordinary child. It provided me with life skills most college freshman lack. I could cook and do laundry and had developed tremendous self-discipline that helped me allocate my time between work, study, and some play. The self-discipline my parents ingrained in me has played a critical role in my lifelong eating and sleeping habits too. I am so grateful for everyone who was instrumental in instilling that in me.

I had a high school track and cross-country coach who would always tell me, "There is no gain without pain." Looking back his words rang true and helped me make sense of my early experiences.

Going forward you need to work on understanding what you store on your memory card. For every memory you have that is holding you back, you can rewrite your story! You can recreate the stories that are keeping you from achieving your goals.

When you cling to a past memory as being "my truth," then you will not change your story. When you don't change your story, nothing in your life changes.

Next Steps

Do you want to learn more about reprogramming your memories? Go to rebootmystories.com for a deep-dive explaining how we are trapped by our memories and how to evaluate and give new meaning to our past.

PART II
OS-ME

A WOMAN IN her late thirties was on her way to a job interview when her car got a flat tire. She was recently divorced after a dozen years of marriage, during which time she had been out of the workforce. She didn't have roadside service and it was before the days of cellphones. She tried to flag down help for twenty minutes.

She was of course dressed in her best suit and high heels and had spent an hour doing her makeup. After realizing no one was going to stop she started to cry. But then she caught herself and decided she was going to figure out how to fix the flat tire herself (although she had never changed a tire before). She struggled to get the jack out of the trunk, jack the car up, and change the tire. At the end, her clothes were dirty, her hands bruised and bloody, and her mascara streaked. But she had triumphed.

From that moment on, her life was changed. She went from feeling helpless to having an undiscovered inner fortitude. She parlayed that attitude into a successful career and a much happier life than before.

She had wiped the victim virus from her brain's operating system and created a new code.

10

HOW OUR BRAIN OPERATING SYSTEM WORKS

In a computer program, there are lines of code that tell the computer what to do. The computer executes each line of code in sequence as directed. In computer programming languages the sequence of commands is important. The same is true with the human operating system.

Here's a synopsis of how the human brain operating system works:

1. Something happens (a "trigger")
2. The event is instantaneously[7] registered in our memory

---

7   · This has to do with quantum physics. Once something happens it is no longer in the present. You can avoid the whole trigger-story-emotion-action-result sequence if you can totally live in the present: just observing and not reacting. This is what meditation is designed to teach you. Turning off your operating system and just observing is a very powerful tool for controlling your life. Chapter 27 discusses meditation.

bank based on some pattern our brain has stored—distorted by memories of the past.

3. We create a story based on these memories, our values, and beliefs.[8]
4. We feel something based on the story we just created.
5. We act (doing nothing is also an action) because of those feelings.
6. Results occur that either reinforce our story or create a new one.
7. Our brain puts the pattern into our memory bank so when something similar happens in the future our brain doesn't have to work as hard to figure it out.

Think of your brain's operating system, or OS-Me, as executing this sequence of processes each time a triggering event happens. Its simplest form is this subroutine that plays over and over all day long:

Create—>Feel—>Act

Remember you are a creator, the one writing the code in your program that generates the stories in your life.

In software, there is something called programming logic. For example, a line of code may say "if Y is true, then go to subroutine 333. If Y is false, go to subroutine 92." A name for this type of code is branching logic.

The events in our life trigger the Y branching where we get to choose which path we go down. As mentioned earlier, attaining new goals requires your personal growth. Growth can only occur when a triggering event—either active or passive—that makes us

---

8 · Technically, your values and beliefs are stories too, so this is a story within a story—a subplot.

uncomfortable occurs in our life. (See Part VI on how (and why) to increase triggering events).

Triggers happen many, many times a day, but we tend to ignore most of them. When you're faced with doing something uncomfortable have you ever told yourself "that's not me?" That uncomfortable feeling is a trigger. And the internal response "that's not me" is just a story that you're telling yourself so that your brain doesn't have to work and grow.

A trigger is something that disrupts our current state and initiates storytelling in our mind. A trigger could be that car that cuts us off in rush hour traffic, the tone someone used when they spoke to us, an eye-roll your spouse used while they were speaking, or even a recollection of a past event. Sometimes even being told that we have the capacity to control our own life can be a trigger!

When reality collides with our current story, we have the opportunity to grow or regress. Living with someone in close quarters creates the most opportunity for this collision with our old stories. The unknown aspect of that human creates chaos in our life.

Why is our first reaction to a trigger to stay stuck?

First, recognize that the brain uses 20 to 30 percent of your body's energy. That's quite a bit of energy for an organ that is only 2 percent of our body weight. Did you know that chess players burn up to six thousand calories a day playing in tournaments while barely moving their bodies? Their brains are working overtime!

The brain uses an estimated 11 to 20 watts/kg of weight whereas the tissue in the rest of the body uses a mere 1.25 watts/kg of body weight. It takes a lot of energy to think! That is why an office worker can come home after a day of work and feel exhausted despite not engaging in physical labor.

The brain is engaged in three elemental functions with competing interests:

- Survive
- Thrive
- Conserve energy

To reduce energy usage the brain takes the infinite complexities of the world and reduces them to simple patterns. Patterns make it easy to "plug and play" whenever a similar situation occurs. This is an evolutionary survival mechanism. For 99.9 percent of human existence finding food was hard work. The brain is constantly engaged in pattern recognition to conserve energy and save itself from danger and starvation.

Our mind creates stories to remember the patterns it observes. It is a simplification process that minimizes calorie usage in the brain and is easy to recall. Pattern recognition is an important skill set. People who can perceive patterns—whether that is identifying a trend in the stock market or perceiving how to seduce someone—often succeed wildly.

A second reason why a trigger causes us to stay stuck is, as Robert Cialdini notes in his book *Influence: The Psychology of Persuasion*, because the mind has a very strong bias to be internally consistent. Even if we know something is wrong or incorrect, we will fight to keep aligned with our previous stories. Poor salespeople struggle to overcome this confirmation bias.

An excellent sales and marketing person uses this knowledge against us to persuade us to buy stuff. He or she will get us to agree with very small statements that are obviously true. As we say yes repeatedly, our internal need to say yes will lead us to agree to buy the product or service for sale. I've used this technique and know it works pretty well.

This confirmation bias is why we often argue that we are 100 percent right when the facts do not support us. We have such a strong tendency to be internally consistent that we often overlook or ignore data in a crisis and will go about our normal activities as if the crisis doesn't exist.

The 2016 US presidential election perfectly illustrates this phenomenon. Before the election one side believed Trump was a genius who could play 3-D chess and outwit his opponents. The other side believed he was a buffoon and a liar.

After the election, the two sides continue to find behaviors that confirm their biases. Often it seems that neither side can understand the other side at all. They each seek out news stories that confirm their biases. Scott Adams called this watching "two movies on one screen."[9]

This is not a recent phenomenon caused by the current president. New York film critic Pauline Kael famously said after Richard Nixon won a forty-nine-state landslide in 1972 that she didn't know anyone who voted for Nixon and couldn't understand his victory.

All this confirmation bias we have is built into stories that we have told ourselves about the other side over a lifetime. Confirmation bias leads us to only associate with people who have the same biases. Associating with non-believers can interfere with our view of reality as it did with Pauline Kael. Today, both sides of the political spectrum continue to find the other appalling.

Beyond personal stories, the brain is plugged into the meta-stories of the human experience. Famed psychologist Carl Jung wrote about stories that all humanity shared. Jung defined this as a "collective unconscious." A present-day Canadian psychologist and fan of Jung, Jordan Peterson, has recorded a series of lectures called *The Psychological Significance of Biblical Stories*. Jordan is excellent at explaining how human experience is impacted by thousands of

---

9   Scott Adams, "Good Example of Our Two-Movie Reality," Scott Adams Says, February 12, 2017, https://www.scottadamssays.com/2017/02/12/good-example-of-our-two-movie-reality/.

years of stories and patterns that our brain uses for understanding the world. You can find Jordan's lectures on YouTube at the time this book was published.

Many of these meta-stories form the basis of the stories of our values and beliefs, of which we are often unconscious. I refer to these as frames and in Part V give some guidance on how to change frames to drive the stories you want.

Even if you claim to be an atheist (and you grew up in the West), your behavior is largely influenced by biblical meta-stories that are prevalent in Western societies. Atheists claim that they can be good people without religion, but the truth is, for those who grew up in the West, it would be impossible to sever the religious influence from their tribal stories.

Stories are our programming language. They are the essential mechanism our brain uses to compress the infinitely complex information from our environment into something we can make sense of. Once the brain adopts a storyline, it takes a large disruption to move from one state to another.

Because the brain is so entrenched in its own patterns and stories, it takes a conscious effort (i.e., energy) to break patterns and move to a new state.

Many self-help books use visualization techniques or repeating a mantra to help overcome destructive patterns. While techniques might help some people, they have never been effective for me. At the core, for me, these gimmicks did not get at the root cause of the reason I would self-sabotage or procrastinate or fail to execute.

When debugging software, trying to hunt and peck through thousands of lines of code to find an error is usually a fruitless endeavor. So engineers employ special debugging software that will systematically analyze where the problematic code may be.

Let's look at a short version of how the human "Debugging Software" works. There are five stages of the process:

1. Clarification – where we examine reality and compare it to our story.
2. Introspection – where we look inside ourselves and examine our motives.
3. Transformation – where we are enlightened.
4. Redirection – where we decide which path to follow.
5. Incentivization – rewarding our system so we continue to grow.

One pass through the special Debugging Software in this book will usually not be enough to break an ingrained pattern. In chemistry, I learned that a calorie is defined as the energy required to raise the temperature of one gram of water by one degree Centigrade. However, to go from 100°C to boiling takes 540 calories. The energy required to change states with no temperature change is much larger than a one-degree temperature rise.

So too is the energy required for you to change states much more than you have given in the past. It will take going through this process several times until you create a new pattern for your brain. Remember, your brain is always looking for patterns and ways to replicate patterns. Each repetition of the process will actually move how and where the trigger occurs for you. For example, we may be mad at the idiot driver who cuts us off the first time it happens. The second time, however, we may be mad at ourselves for not paying attention to traffic appropriately. The third time it happens we may recall some turmoil from childhood that affects our ability to deal with the stress of bad traffic. At last, we may be at peace and wish the other driver well and blame no one or nothing.

This is due to the process of feedback. All the systems in our body depend on getting information returned about whether a certain process is working or not. For example, our bodies are driven to control blood sugar levels. If levels get too high or too low we can get quite ill or die. Our body's' feedback loop measures sugar levels and signals the pancreas how much insulin to excrete.

Feedback loops are also a big part of any computer program and our brain uses feedback endlessly in evaluating the environment and figuring out what to do. When an event occurs the brain scans all our memories for a similar event, a pattern. The brain instantly makes a complex calculation trading off energy conservation versus growth versus delivering a dopamine hit. Then it transmits the okay to react again similarly.

Feedback loops are why people used to believe that as we grew older we were stuck with old patterns of behavior. Scientists used to think the repetition of these loops firing the same neurons in our brains created pathways, much like river valleys, that were hard to change. New research indicates that our brains are quite plastic (malleable) and these pathways can be remade at any age.

Let's discuss how important feedback loops are to the way the world looks.

11

FEEDBACK LOOPS AND THE 80/20 PRINCIPLE

Do you ever wonder why only a handful of people seem to have great success? Italian economist Vilfredo Pareto discovered a phenomenon called the 80/20 Principle or Pareto's Law. Pareto lived in the seventeenth century and documented how wealth was distributed. No matter how often money was redistributed it continually reorganized so that in a short time 20 percent of the people would always end up controlling 80 percent of the wealth.

Pareto found that it didn't matter which country or economic system or time period he observed, the distribution of money and wealth was always the same.

Pareto's Law is not a theory but an actual observation about how the world works. Billionaire venture capitalist Richard Koch wrote the excellent book *The 80/20 Principle* explaining this in detail.

This observation by Pareto applies not only to money but also to many natural and even artificial phenomena. For example, if your closet contains one hundred shirts you most likely wear twenty shirts 80 percent of the time. If you have a hundred friends, you spend 80 percent of your time with just twenty of them. This ratio even applies to smaller subgroups. Of the time you spend with those twenty friends you probably spend 80 percent of that time with just four friends!

These numbers are not exact of course but Pareto's distribution follows a curve like the one below:

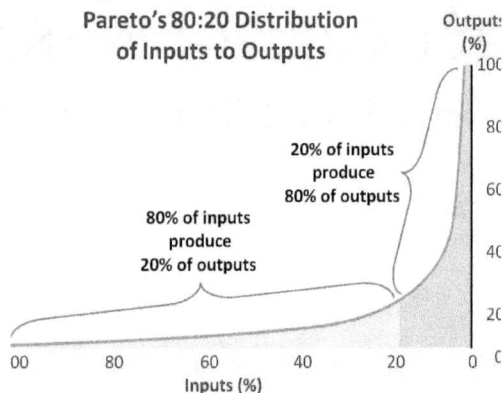

Pareto's 80:20 Distribution of Inputs to Outputs

20% of inputs produce 80% of outputs

80% of inputs produce 20% of outputs

Inputs (%)

This may look familiar to those who watched the news during the 2020 COVID-19 pandemic as we were inundated with exponential curves. No matter where or when an outbreak of the disease started, the curves all looked the same.

Those without knowledge of this fundamental principle often express envy and resentment toward those who have money, health, or lots of friends. Sometimes they even grovel in conspiracy theories. They see themselves as helpless victims of big corporations or secret societies.

The key to understanding why this happens is feedback loops. When I studied control theory in college, it was in regard to systems that were going out of control. Like wildfires or nuclear explosions or pandemics, runaway reactions are also unwanted. As an engineer, I spent my time studying ways to control feedback loops. It never occurred to me that creating a runaway reaction could be used in a positive way to build skills.

Feedback loops or habits reinforce or amplify whatever systems or behaviors that are running. If you are trying to set off an atomic bomb (God forbid), you want to start the chain reaction or feedback loop to get that event going.

However, if you are trying to improve your life in some manner, then you want to start a chain reaction of good habits that will move you toward positive growth. We do this by reviewing our stories to understand why we do what we do.

This will help you to not be jealous or envy other people's successes. (When we envy others we are telling ourselves we are powerless to create similar results.)

The next time the same or a similar trigger happens, the information fed back to our brain's operating system (the revelation or the reinforcement) amplifies the results.

When we recognize how a trigger occurred, our brain imprints a new pattern in our mind. The revelation causes the feedback loop to reinforce our story positively. We get better and better at whatever skill we use to evaluate and respond when we are triggered.

When there is no revelation then the brain finds no new patterns and reinforces the previous story in a negative manner. Old habits and ideas are bolstered creating the downward spiral as shown in the illustration below.

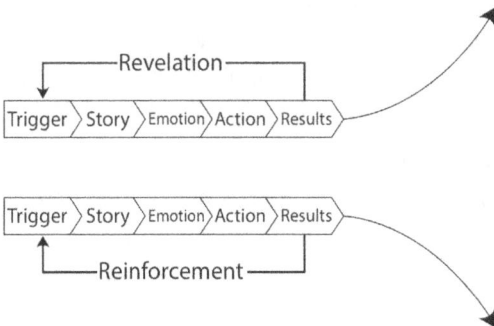

This growth is not linear; it is exponential, like compound interest. Compound interest grows very slowly in the beginning then suddenly it delivers huge results.

There is a good exercise to envision this: try doubling a penny every day for a month and see what happens! For example, you will have two cents on the second day, four cents on the third day, and so on. By the end of the first week, you will have only $0.64. Yet after thirty-one days you will have $10.7 million! That is why anything you are trying to get better at seems so hard when you start.

The amount of new knowledge we discover as each iteration of a feedback loop occurs determines our rate of positive growth. Learning to view results correctly is critical to our success in any endeavor. It is important to understand operating system bugs that keep you from seeing results accurately, which I discuss in Part IV.

Whether the feedback loop is positive or negative depends on whether we are using our frontal cortex or our amygdala to analyze the results. The frontal cortex will give us revelations; our amygdala will reinforce old patterns.

An extreme example of a negative feedback loop is road rage. I read about an incident where one man cut off another. The man who was cut off chased down the other man. They came to a stoplight and their anger accelerated to the point where both drew out their handguns and shot each other to death.

That was a bad day! It's likely that both men had experienced lots of triggers that day and probably over the past few weeks and months, like the protagonist ready to jump off the bridge in Chapter 2. Even if one of them had resolved previous triggers it would have broken the chain reaction.

A review of our stories sets us up to get an epiphany, which increases the probability of our success exponentially. This natural phenomenon prevails in many human activities, not only in the area of money. We can use it to improve our relationships, our musical or sports skills, our health, or any situation where we feel uncomfortable.

Personal trainer Tim Grover wrote a book called *Relentless: From Good to Great to Unstoppable* in which he describes how Michael Jordan used this process to transform from being average to the greatest basketball player. Jordan spent day after day working on the same skills, forcing himself to continue even when he did not see immediate results.

Here is where it gets confusing because the nature of reality is impossible to assess. I may see "reality" as one thing and you may see it as the complete opposite. The only way to observe reality is to evaluate the results of our experiments. Whenever we create a story we are experimenting with reality. It is like a user interface. The user interface serves as a guide about how to react to experiments. Like any science experiment, our stories produce results. It is essential that we can critically evaluate the results of our stories. Here's where being honest with ourselves is so important—and looking at the long term. If I rob a bank because I need money, I may tell myself that I got the result I wanted (money), but the long-term consequences (jail and a felony record) may not be so good.

Acting on your view of reality will produce different results than acting on my view. When we are honest, we can review if our reality produced the results we want or not. That is, do we like the results we produced? Are they good for us? Do they satisfy our long-term needs on the Maslow hierarchy?

If the results of our actions are not positively reinforcing what we want, then change the story. This may involve setting a new goal and also putting a new system in place to make sure we don't go down the same path.

Many people struggle with procrastination and numerous books are available on that subject. We know that procrastination is a progeny of inner fear. So we tell ourselves a story that creates fear and stops us from acting. The Debugging Software helps us dissect the story that causes us to fear and help us resolve our issues.

Here's where positive thinking and visualization can help. If you don't get the results you want and think "I can do this, let me revise my story" versus "I don't think I can do this," you will have different feedback loops.

Two important points to remember:

1. There is a delay between your actions and long-term term results.
2. Doing small things repeatedly over time is very powerful and creates a compounding result that grows exponentially.

In the world's encounter with the coronavirus COVID-19 in 2020 each country where someone initiated the infection, there seemed like a long period where nothing happened. Then all at once, the hospitals were overwhelmed with sick patients as the cases grew exponentially. The growth was so rapid that many countries shut down their economies to try to mitigate the disease spread.

The world's expert on persuasion, Robert Cialdini's observation about commitment and consistency is based on the fact that our brain likes patterns. We create new patterns by making small, incremental changes toward our goals and rewarding ourselves for the small wins. Taking small steps consistently reinforces the pattern. Over time we build a new pattern that results in this exponential growth.

Be patient waiting for results and impatient with your actions.

When we think this way, we can proactively create the life we want and stop envying other people. Of course, crap will happen to us. But we can change how we deal with it. The more we expand

and grow personally by using the techniques in Part VI, the less it will affect us.

You will also realize there is no need to be jealous of other people's success since you now know how they did it. To believe otherwise is to deny the role we have played in not using our creative abilities to generate better circumstances in our life.

If we have a victim story in our mind, we may argue that others succeeded because of their race or their power or privilege or luck.

I lived in Appalachia for twenty years. There are plenty of poor people there. And there were many dysfunctional families and drug issues as well. Looking back and thinking about this in the context of the 80/20 Principle it is easy to see why.

Generation after generation of people did the same thing and got the same results. The local tribes continually reinforced stories of poverty and hopelessness. Families perpetuated a pattern of failure, creating more failure. Stories were reinforced and repeated endlessly. People felt oppressed and victimized and so they did not take any actions to change their circumstances.

If you look you will find that "lucky" people are reading *The Seven Habits of Highly Successful People* by Stephen Covey and the "unlucky" ones read about how the 9/11 terrorist attacks were an inside job.

Telling ourselves a story that everything is racist or sexist is not empowering. However true we may believe it to be, this storyline keeps us stuck. No redistribution of money or power or privilege will fix us.

Many people with victim stories try to shortcut the 80/20 Principle by advocating for socialism or communism. However, nature cannot be denied. What happens in societies that punish meritocratic wealth creation is that:

1. The people who are good at creating wealth leave the country, and

2. The people with the weapons use the 80/20 Principle to consolidate their power.

The rulers become the new 1 percent and steal the wealth that remains.

The people who supported the revolution are left worse off than before. That is why Vladimir Lenin called the masses "useful idiots." He fed on people's tendency to play the victim.

Lenin used feedback loops against the people he pretended he was saving. Charlatans and marketing experts all understand feedback loops and how to use them to manipulate us. If you are unaware of this you will spend your life doing others bidding. Let's look at how these feedback loops work.

12

PROGRAMMING LANGUAGE COMMANDS

OFTEN IN COMPUTER programming, a certain sequence must be followed to make the feedback loop work correctly. Here is a fundamental feedback loop that our mind uses:

1. We create stories about events based on our memories plus our interpretation of reality, which are based on facts but also on:

   - Our experiences, which are clouded by our stories about our values and beliefs.

   - Experiences of others (from friends, books, movies, etc.), which fog up our memories.

   - Cultural stories of our tribal group (religious, ethnic, family, gender, political and/or racial groups we identify with).

   - The meta-stories that human beings seem to have in common no matter the culture.

2. Our emotions flow from the stories we create. If you've ever felt that you can't control your emotions, you are correct! You actually don't! We control our emotions only indirectly from a story we created. We cry at movies because the story elicited an emotion from us. The paper and ink used to create a book won't make us sad, but the story can.

Ever been at a funeral crying over the loss of a loved one when someone starts telling funny stories about events that happened with that loved one? Tears turn to laughter and our sadness turns to joy about treasured moments shared.

Telling stories is a powerful path to control your emotions.

This is a major obstacle many people have in understanding their stories. They believe they cannot control their emotions or that someone else is causing their emotions. Neither of those statements is true. Our emotions only flow from our internal story.

I remember going to a marriage counselor many years ago. She thought she was teaching us the proper way to argue. She instructed us to use the phrase, "When you do X, you make me feel Y" instead of shouting accusations at each other. This seems logical but is quite false. This never made sense to me. I remember hearing my ex-wife use this phrase, and I would get angrier.

No one can make us feel anything, and we are
not responsible for how anyone else feels.

Psychologists who promote that type of conflict resolution are actually disempowering patients. The rule of thumb is: if you require someone else to act or say things a certain way to be able to be at peace, then you lose power and the ability to fix yourself.

Don't get me wrong. We can definitely hurt others with our words. However, this is distinct from the story the other person tells themselves about our evil behavior and the subsequent feelings they have.

Victor Frankl was a Jew who spent years in a German concentration camp where death was everywhere. It was obvious the guards were trying to inflict harm and death on the prisoners. But Victor found a way to create a story where he was not a victim despite the horror surrounding him. The prison guards, no matter what they did to him, did not control his emotions because they could not control his stories.

3. Our emotions dictate our actions. Remember the fight, flight, freeze, and fawn reactions the amygdala creates in response to a threat? Freezing or procrastinating is also an action. All actions—both positive and negative—come from the amygdala. The frontal cortex observes and thinks.

4. Our actions produce results. Most people pay limited attention to the results their stories produce or just to the results they agree with. Confirmation bias often blinds us to the real results. When we are aware of our internal biases, we can use the results to help create a new story or reinforce an old one.

5. The results of our actions give us information our brain stores and uses as feedback for the next time a similar event occurs. The brain is looking for a pattern.

Our brain compiles memories for future use. When it sees a pattern it creates a story from those memories. The stories are our brain's programming language. Our brain uses feedback loops to build patterns, reinforcing old ones or starting better ones.

We create most of our stories passively or even unconsciously from previous patterns our brain has stored. Our brain is creating these stories in milliseconds, so it's not a conscious process unless we interfere. This is why some "experts" think our lives are predetermined.

But the truth is that we **can** choose to create stories actively.

The creation of the story is the primary purpose of our operating system (OS-Me). Actively crafting stories rather than letting our brain use old patterns to create them puts us in command of our OS-Me. The subsequent emotions generated will drive our actions.

When we energetically desire something and set all our attention on achieving it, we are proactively crafting a new story. But sometimes we don't seem to get the outcome we want.

Why is that?

There is another powerful command language at work that overrides our desire to change. I call it the "I am" story command.

Self-help books often tell you to create "I am" statements about what you want to be. Whether they work or not depends on recognition of what is going on with your subconscious beliefs.

Ever go to a party or meet someone new and one of the first questions is, "What do you do?" Our automatic response seems to be to announce, "I'm a (fill in the blank with whatever job you hold and/or a belief you have)." "I'm an accountant" or "I'm a gay fashion designer" or "I'm a vegan activist" are stories.

You are not your story.

We have actively spent our whole life creating and nurturing a story about ourselves. It is so part of us that we don't consciously consider it as a story. In your "I am" story you are like a fish in water, unaware that it is even a story.

The "I am" story uses confirmation bias to keep us entrenched in our present situation. That story includes not just what we do but other characteristics, such as, "I am shy" or "I am a loser," "I am clumsy," "I am sad," or "I am boring."

Our brain executes "I am" command statements dozens of times a day either consciously or unconsciously reinforcing our beliefs and behaviors.

In order for a new "I am" statement to pull us out of our current situation, it has to be congruent with our internal stories. Some people are capable of self-hypnosis and creating "I am" statements to overwhelm their self-doubt.

For most of us, these declarations don't work due to our need for internal consistency with our old "I am" beliefs. People will cite that they feel like a phony when using an "I am" statement to convince themselves that they are some desired state. Our statement must be consistent with our internal beliefs about ourselves and what is possible. We tend to think of persuasion as something salespeople do to us, but it is also needed for internal change.

Mohammad Ali famously said of himself, "I am the greatest." No doubt he believed it, but he was really saying it as much for himself as for the world. The Debugging Software will help you find the internal consistency that allows you to make a new "I am" statement.

If your current "I am" story is getting you the results you want in life, then continue on. If that story is interfering with the results you want, then learn how to actively create a new one. Again, you are *not* your story!

To be clear, using the phrase "I am"[10] is one of the most powerful storytelling command languages available to us. The phrase actualizes the most potent results. But if our "I am" statement is negative, it can also freeze us from taking action to change due to our need to stay internally consistent.

Be careful with your self-talk. Use it with deliberate consideration about what you really desire. Let's look at how you can turn your storyline into producing goals and results

---

10 · Even God used that phrase describing Himself to Moses in the burning bush

13

PROGRAM RESULTS AND GIGO

EARLIER I PROPOSED this formula for getting results:

Goals + Systems + Actions = Results

We now know that actions flow from emotions, which originate with the story we tell ourselves. So getting the results we want requires correctly defining all three variables of this equation. Goals create the stories. Systems place constraints on the story and reward outcomes we desire. What we are doing is trying to craft new tribal mores for ourselves with a system. In the Debugging Software, you will be asked to consider what results you desire. Consider these questions as you evaluate your options:

- Do I have a goal or purpose for this situation or am I winging it?
- Do I have a system in place that will help me achieve this goal or is my life chaotic in this event?

- Is my story about the event aligned with the goal and did it follow my system?

When I was studying computer programming in college, the first acronym I learned was GIGO—garbage in garbage out. This also applies to how we program our brains.

Every story we create has consequences. We cannot ignore them. Sometimes they are unintended outcomes. If we really want to change our stories, we should consider all the by-products of what we do as we analyze what has happened.

Analyzing the results of our actions correctly is pivotal to creating the change we desire. Letting the chips fall where they may, allows our amygdala to run our brains. There are many times when we fool ourselves about the results of our actions. Our minds have a built-in confirmation bias, which causes us to see only repercussions that back up our pre-conceived beliefs. We ignore results that contradict our biases.

Seeing the fruit of our actions clearly, requires absolute honesty with ourselves. Often our confirmation biases keep us blind to what is obvious to others. So sometimes it takes the observations of another person who does not share our biases to see results clearly. It's also important that the other person doesn't share our tribal affiliation if our storyline is related to tribal issues. For example, if we have a story about relationships with the opposite sex, a same-sex friend might have an indistinguishable bias when interpreting the results of our actions.

We cannot look at results in a vacuum, however. They must be measured against our purpose or goals. You must be assessing them versus your goals.

Maybe you were triggered by someone cutting you off in traffic and you think, "What does that have to do with my goals?" What if one of your goals is to improve your health? Getting angry and causing your blood pressure to increase is contra that goal.

My father told me to count to ten whenever someone triggered me and I wanted to say something inappropriate. This is an example of a simple system you could use in the traffic situation.

Every triggering event is an opportunity to grow in order to get results we really want in life. To create new stories as you learn to deal with what triggers you go through the Debugging Software. This process is extremely effective, but it requires honesty. And the first person we tend to lie to is always ourselves. Many people just don't want to be honest with themselves. It is easier to believe something that isn't true if it confirms our inner biases than to face the possibility that we are wrong.

In the computer metaphor, lying is the garbage data that we feed back to our brains. When our brains have garbage data and use that data to create a new story, we get unexpected or unwanted results.

If you wonder why your life is not changing, bad data could be the answer.

**Until we stop lying to ourselves, we will
stay stuck with our current story!**

PART III
CORRECTING THE CODE

Seen on Facebook:

Her Diary:
Tonight I thought my husband was acting weird. We had made plans to meet at a nice restaurant for dinner. I was shopping with my friends all day long. I thought he was upset at the fact that I was a bit late, but he made no comment on it. The conversation wasn't flowing, so I suggested we go somewhere quiet so we could talk. He agreed but didn't say much. I asked him what was wrong. He said, "Nothing." I asked him if it was my fault that he was upset. He said he wasn't upset. It had nothing to do with me and not to worry about it.

On the way home I told him I loved him. He smiled slightly and kept driving. I can't explain his behavior. I don't know why he didn't say, "I love you too." When we got home, I felt as if I had lost him completely, as if he wanted nothing to do with me anymore. He just sat there quietly and watched TV.

He continued to seem distant and absent. Finally, with silence all around us, I decided to go to bed. About fifteen minutes later he came to bed. But I still felt his thoughts were distracted and somewhere else. He fell asleep. I cried. I don't know what to do. I'm almost sure his thoughts are with someone else. My life is a disaster.

His diary:
Boat motor won't start . . . can't figure out why.

14

THE DEBUGGING SOFTWARE[11]

As I'VE MENTIONED before, the purpose of the debugging process is to train your brain to use its frontal cortex rather than the amygdala to evaluate triggers or events in our lives. Think of this as programming our brain to not overreact and infect our hard drive just because we clicked on a spam email with a mysterious link.

Often we seek advice or counsel—a savior if you will—to solve our problems. However, most of the answers in the diagnosis stage will come from our inner voice. Our inner voice will almost always reveal the truth. Try to be still and quiet your mind as you

---

11   The basis of this process is Byron Katie's "The Work" and Garret J. White's "The Stack"

go through this process. Take deep breaths and listen to your inner voice. Tell yourself that you have the wisdom to change yourself.

Start by examining something that triggered you today. (As you gain experience working through this process you can go back to events that triggered you in your past, but for now, examine something more current.) Re-examine the stories you told yourself at that moment. This can give you a very deep personal under-standing of yourself way beyond what any psychologist can give you. There is a story behind every emotion you feel. When you see a tiger you may think you didn't have time to create a story, your fear was just generated by the amygdala. But your brain had seen this pattern before and created a story that your life was in danger. You may not be aware of it until you consciously look to reveal it. That is the purpose of this process.

I've used this process to reprogram what I thought about my childhood and how I see my parents and my ex-wife. I have even become grateful for everything that has happened to me.

I summarized this process in the last chapter, but now it is time to look more closely at the five sections: clarification, intro-spection, transformation, redirection and incentivization. As I walk you through the steps, be ready to answer some questions and write down your answers.

Just thinking about them won't have as much of an impact in your early attempts learning this process as writing them down. As you become more experienced you will be able to go through this process mentally.

కⅆ

1. Clarification

This step will bring us clarity about what the problem is. Problems can only be solved when they are well defined. One of the traits I learned as an engineer is that correctly describing the problem is

80 percent of the solution. In this step, we look at the facts and attempt to eliminate our opinions, biases, and beliefs about what the other person is thinking. Note that throughout this process, none of the questions are about the other person. Your outcome from this section should be clarity about what the problem is.

Explain what triggered you.

What is a trigger? It's an event that disrupts our state of mind. That event could be something happening now, or it could have happened years ago. It's important to identify and name such an event because it has power over us. By naming a triggering event, we reveal the truth and take control and stop feeling like a victim. In our politically correct culture, people avoid naming things because the truth is so uncomfortable, and few want to face the truth.

Think about a triggering event in your life that you can examine and to which you will refer when answering the questions below. Note that an event can also be a thought we have about something. The recollection of old memories could also trigger you. What happened that caused you to create a story? What actual facts about this event can you detail?

In the story of our protagonist there were many events that triggered him during his day:

- Thoughts about the crummy town he lived in.
- Thoughts about the lousy house he lived in.
- The sound of his children screaming.
- The refusal of the noxious, rich businessman to help him.
- A broken part of the stairway in the old house he lived in that caused him to stumble.
- His wife telling him to leave.
- The auditor who told him that money was missing.

- His business partner who he suspected was responsible for the lost money.
- The man that punched him in the bar.
- His thoughts of the failing business he hated.
- The recollection of the dreams he had passed up.
- The thoughts of a God that ignored his prayers.

Like our protagonist, often when there is a major event, like the loss of money in his case, multiple other issues come to the surface. As we react to each new trigger the results pile up in our subconscious and are ready to explode. For example, often when people are diagnosed with a major medical problem, issues with their spouse or parents or a childhood trauma come to the forefront and trigger them. I recall when I was very young my grandfather died. Upon hearing the news, I had no external reaction. Later that day I started crying over a small, inconsequential situation about sandwiches. My dad yelled at me for crying over this and not for his father. The triggers we notice are often the result of accumulated stresses that have snowballed. It's obvious the primary triggering event was my grandfather's death, not a sandwich.

As you work on the Debugging Software if you find that you have multiple triggers, you should rank them. Many would think that addressing the thorniest issues first would be the way to go. But the likely result would be for you to freeze and not move forward due to the high level of fear about revealing the truth. So pick some easy ones to work on until you become familiar with the process. Once you have confidence and your reward system is working, then tackle harder issues.

Each of the triggers in the list above held power over our protagonist making him feel victimized. Just like bugs in a software program, you have to work through all of them to make your software run smoothly.

If you think that the trigger was a feeling—anxiety, fear, worry, doubt or anger—write that down for now.

Who or what is the focus of your anger?

Our story flows from the amygdala where (unless we've trained our brains) we react reflexively. This means that our first primal reaction is anger. You may have trained yourself to repress your anger and only experience a general anxiety, or you may react by getting raging mad.

Most people don't realize that they carry around a good deal of anger because they believe, consciously or subconsciously, that they are victims. Men are often taught to suppress their emotions. In Chapter 8 we saw that Dostoevsky believed that we all are collectively responsible for all the evil in the world. This idea begins with the realization of a collective anger.

One of the ways to heal from this anger is to admit that our first reaction to this trigger may be to hurt the "other" that we believe has hurt us. This is our hidden dark side. Who or what is this other that we seek to blame for being triggered?

What would you do if you let your anger consume you? Sometimes we get angry with ourselves or angry at a world we have no control over. You may be mad at God, the universe or the government. I've gotten angry at inanimate objects—tools, cars, and especially my computer. The key to debugging our brain's software is to admit we have a primordial response to triggers and not pretend the anger doesn't exist. Men are especially good at trying to hide their anger or pretend it doesn't exist.

Our protagonist says he was quite angry. But who was he angry with? Was he angry with his father for dying? Was he mad at his mother for needing his support? Was he angry at his brother who should have taken over the business but instead married, moved to Buffalo, and essentially abandoned him? He may have been mad at the situation with his business.

Sorting these kinds of things out in your mind can give you clarity when you work on alternative stories.

Recently a sibling told me that they resented me for abandoning them when I left home as a teenager and they were still quite young.

That suggestion triggered me.

Inside I wanted to yell, "I changed and washed your stinky diapers and sacrificed my childhood to take care of you and this is the gratitude I get?" When I analyzed my reaction, I had to ask myself, "Am I still angry about my childhood?"

What is the story you told yourself? Is it true? Are we 100 percent certain?

Is your mind stuck on staying internally consistent with previous stories? Is confirmation bias keeping you from seeing other facts about what happened? Remember we have an incredible need to confirm how we see things. Solving problems requires stepping outside our worldview.

There is a great deal of ambiguity in the world and being 100 percent convinced of any event can create huge blind spots in us. Max Planck, a famous physicist, said that science advances one death at a time. The truth is that even brilliant scientists are blinded by their confirmation bias and only upon their death can science advance.

If for the trigger you chose to examine, you wrote down a feeling, now is the time to clarify the root cause of that feeling. Our brain is referencing stored patterns and creating stories, which generate the emotion. Part of ridding ourselves of a destructive cycle is finding the truth of what is going on. When we tell ourselves we cannot control our emotions or let our emotions drive our decisions, we are relinquishing our power. Emotions are as much in our control as our actions are.

As an example, think back to when we were in quarantine to protect ourselves from the COVID-19 virus in 2020. Many of us spent the day listening to the prognosticators tell us how many people were going to die and looking at charts of the spread of the pandemic. Many people felt anxious. If you felt anxious, news about the disease and potential for death created a fear in your brain and generated a story that you or someone you loved was going to get sick or die. Those stories generated the anxiety. In this step, we intend to break the cycle of anxiety.

Our protagonist told himself he was likely to go to prison and lose everything he owned. He told himself that he was worth more dead than alive. These were not facts—just his opinions. The facts were that a bank auditor found that our protagonist's firm was missing some money.

Our protagonist filled himself with stories of bankruptcy and loss of face and hopelessness. The facts did not support his story.

My story was that I didn't feel I had harmed my siblings or abandoned them in any way. I remembered that I had frequently returned home for vacations and on school breaks. I had taken care of my siblings when they were most vulnerable, and I felt they should treat me with respect. Our stories were different, but both stories can provide valuable information for our analysis.

What real evidence do you have to prove your story is true?

Our stories often use mind reading as evidence. Mind reading is when you think you know what someone else is thinking. Don't ever think you know someone else's thoughts. If we are sure our story is true even without any real evidence, we might be hallucinating. I'll cover mind reading more in Chapter 15.

Our protagonist got into a fight in a bar because he was mind reading the motives of someone else. He was angry and upset because his partner lost all their money. To make sense of everything, he assumed his sick child's teacher was out to hurt his family.

Likewise, I assumed that when I left home for college and came home on breaks, I was a good big brother. Apparently, I was only a good big brother in my own mind. We have to take more perspectives into consideration than our own. I argued my memory was perfect against all other evidence in order to remain internally consistent. Arguing from distant memories is not a position of strength.

What feelings did you have when you believed your story to be true?

While your initial reaction to the trigger may have been anger, there are often other feelings that arise. By documenting the other emotions we can see how connected our feelings are to the story we created. Each emotion may have a slightly different story connected to it than anger. This is an important link to establish so that we can learn to stop blaming others for our feelings.

Each feeling may have different levels:

- Rage, anger and annoyance
- Loathing, disgust, boredom
- Grief, sadness, pensiveness
- Terror, fear, apprehension
- Contempt, anxiety, submission or disproval

Of course, there are good emotions that trigger us as well. We usually don't fret over having positive emotions, but you can also use this process to analyze what does make us happy. I am not covering that now because most people are focused on fixing themselves. Later you can see if you can figure out how to create more feedback loops based on positive emotions.

This step is critical because so many people believe their feelings drive their behaviors, and so they are focused on their feelings and how others hurt their feelings.

There is a movement on college campuses to create "safe spaces." These are areas where students are sheltered from ideas contrary to their own. When we try to protect our operating system by blocking new ideas, then we are subordinate to someone else and vulnerable. Blocking new ideas is like trying to improve our immune system by living inside a plastic bubble. Our beliefs must be exposed to new ideas just like our immune system needs to be exposed to new germs in order to thrive. Unfortunately, for students so insecure that they cannot be in a room with someone of the opposite opinion no one can save them, not even the "wise" college administrators who try to placate them.

The inability to understand where emotions originate and to blame others for our feelings is a huge block to healing ourselves. I've been in several intimate relationships where one party declares that "you hurt my feelings." The aggrieved party feels that they were hurt intentionally.

When we feel triggered by someone and assign intentionality to their actions we are engaged in mind reading. If someone says something that you find offensive, it's likely that there are two aspects that may be true:

a. You are fabricating a story about this person's intentions.

b. What this person said is "poking" a Me story you have.

Whatever their intention may have been, focusing on that does not help us. Understanding our reaction gives us the insight we need to control our OS-Me.

When my siblings accused me of abandoning the family I got angry. The accusation triggered my image of myself as a caretaker.

After all, I had taken care of my siblings for years, took care of two different families, and took care of work associates in my work laboratory.

The accusation hurt me. After all, I saw myself as the most responsible one out of all my siblings. I was the firstborn, the one in charge of making sure everyone was safe, fed, and protected. I also felt sadness that I had missed something by not being as much a part of the family as my siblings. I sensed my role as the pseudo-parent had forced me to be separate from my siblings.

What did you do when your story was attacked?

When someone contradicts one of the stories we have about ourselves or accuses us of being different from how we see ourselves, we feel threatened. Think when your story was challenged and notice how your feelings caused you to take some kind of action. Many people set goals and then don't take any action toward those goals and wonder why they didn't achieve their goals. It's because their emotions dictated their actions.

For example, we may set a goal to make ten sales calls a day. However, we have a story that people will reject our sales pitch, so we are afraid to make the calls. There are numerous books on the market to address procrastination issues, but procrastination is simply a freeze reaction.

Sometimes people try to will an action with a strong primordial scream (a technique I've read in other books and tried myself). However, their story of doubt creates an underlying fear that causes them to keep their foot on the brakes.

We can use this knowledge that stories pave the way to emotions in the future to avoid responses we don't want or take actions we desire, or we can be overcome by our emotions that are caused by the stories we tell ourselves.

Our protagonist chose the latter and became triggered by

the auditor's statement of fact that he lost the company's deposit money. He allowed a story he told himself (that he might go to prison and lose everything he had) to create feelings of anger and fear. As a consequence, he yelled at his wife and children, got in a fight with a man in a bar, and at last stood on the edge of a bridge ready to jump into an icy river below.

My actions when my story was challenged were to argue with my sibling that my memory was superior and to then withdraw.

What were the results of your actions?

The results can be internal to you as well as external. An internal result may be a surge of adrenalin you felt, an increased heart rate or a wave of sadness. Externally it could be the emotion you provoked in someone else or a physical result (like the road rage warriors who shot each other). They can be short term and long term. Write down as many results as you can observe. Are those the results you wanted for yourself and/or others?

The results of our protagonist's actions were that his wife told him to leave; he got drunk in a bar and got punched in the face.

The results of my actions were that nothing was resolved. Both parties left the discussion with the same story as they had at the beginning. Quite possibly we were both more convinced of the correctness of our positions as we were before.

Will the current story give you the results you want for yourself and others?

When someone cuts you off in traffic, what do you want for yourself and the other person? Will showing your middle finger to them or pressing on your horn teach them a lesson or just escalate the problem? What will it do to your blood pressure—not to mention the safety of you and your passengers—if you react badly?

Deep down our protagonist did not want to lose his family, his reputation, or his life.

In conclusion, asking yourself these questions will help bring clarification to your situation from an external perspective. Now it's time to look at things introspectively.

2. Introspection

The first section focused on the outside, now it's time to turn to our inside world. A trigger pokes us because there is an unresolved issue in our life that needs our attention. Until we resolve that issue, triggers will continue to generate a reaction in us. We don't hold grudges against people who trigger us. They're just who we project our feelings on. The underlying issue lies in the past. In our hearts, we believe our anger can change the past, but that is not possible.

When we consider the underlying issue behind our reaction, it's easy to see the focus of our anger is not at all the other person. If you look at your internal thoughts and feelings, you will become aware of the root causes of your problems. Then you will better understand where your victim status comes from.

This is the most important section of this book. We either suffer to improve or suffer because we won't. Running away from pain is worse than the pain itself. Skip it at your own peril.

What is your Me story?

The first story we usually tell is not the whole story. There is always some internal, often subconscious, story in play. Call it the Me story. What is the Me version of this story we just told? That is, what story is it we tell that gives us the most reward?

Humans are very self-absorbed creatures. Almost everything we do and think about revolves around how it impacts us.

This is undoubtedly an evolutionary self-preservation mechanism. Even young children's first impulses are selfish. They focus on me and mine. When strangers approached our ancestors (or approach us today) the amygdala had to evaluate whether there was a threat. The impulse to preserve oneself when threatened is quite strong.

In the clarification section, we focused on anger. Anger grows from the seed of hidden fear. Your Me story could be the result of some deep emotional yearning for love, some pain you remember, or an insecurity you feel, but it's always fear of something. These are often very old memories that are subconsciously poking us. (Unsurprisingly they are often related to interactions with our parents or very early childhood experiences).[12]

We often use our anger to project our inner psyche onto others. The first step in healing is to learn how we use projection to cast our internal stories outside us.

Think about what your story—the Me story coming from your amygdala—is giving you. What is the payoff? Our original stories are like the tip of an iceberg, while the Me story is the 90 percent that is below the surface.

Me stories break down into four primary areas.

The first type of Me stories are victim stories. If the genesis of the Me story developed when we were very young, then we likely were a victim. Recall that our helpless nature in our first years made us all victims, so you likely have a residue victim story. However, as adults, we have the capacity to reexamine these stories and stop playing a victim. We are no longer children operating in an adult world. Our brain has now developed the aptitude to reason and give new meaning to past events.

People cling to their victim stories their whole life to avoid taking responsibility for their actions. People also hang on to

---

12   Some assert that 90 percent of our psychosis comes before age ten. See the book *Homecoming: Reclaiming and Healing Your Inner Child* by John Bradshaw for insights into healing those hurts.

victim stories that happened hundreds of years ago to their tribe (race or gender or religion), which are no longer valid. There are tribes of people that hate each other for some event that happened five hundred or a thousand years ago. The hatred is just perpetuated from generation to generation without any recent reason.

The second type of Me stories are selfish, entitled tales where we are the center of the universe. They are the stories of our inner child yelling, "Mine," "Me, me, me!"

The people who tell themselves these stories tend to be very narcissistic—always wanting to be the center of attention. In Chapter 17 I discuss drama queens in depth.

When I was just out of college I visited a nude beach on the Caribbean island of Martinique. A man on the beach was surrounded by a large crowd of mostly women who were gawking at him. This was before the age of body piercing, and he had pierced his genitals. Apparently, he wanted to be the center of attention that day.

A third type of Me story revolves around our self-obsessed inadequacies. This type of story relates to seeing ourselves as incompetent. When we are young, we see the world of adults doing things that we wish to do. When we try to do adult-type tasks we fail and develop comparison stories. When we compare our deficiencies with someone who is more skilled, we feel inferior. Comparison stories are a great reason to create depression stories about our life as I discuss in Chapter 20. Just thinking about someone more competent often will trigger us.

The fourth Me story relates to the I am story. For example, suppose you have a script around your appearance like "I am ugly." Presume you are romantically interested in someone, and they ignore you. This triggers you to run a story that the other person is a jerk or misogynist because they ignored you. In reality, that person not paying attention to you could do so for dozens of reasons. But the real reason you feel triggered is your I am story regarding your appearance. I suffered this kind of trigger for decades thanks to my childhood neighbor.

"You can often identify Me stories by finding the controlling trigger. A control trigger is a statement like "What's wrong with me?" or "Money doesn't grow on trees." We may not even be aware of the controlling trigger when another trigger occurs. Our tribal group infected us with most of these types of sparks or triggers.

Our protagonist may have been triggered by his story of the rich businessman. For example, he might believe an I am story like "I am a failure because my business never made any profit." He could have had a controlling trigger about how evil rich people were. Or he could have had victim stories about why he felt he had to run the business. Was he trying to be the good son to his mom after his father's death? Was he trying to be the town's savior and protect the people in the town from the rich "greedy" old businessman?

I often have had Me stories similar to our protagonist. For example, my first wife and I would argue about money. I would blame her for spending too much. Internally though, my Me story was dominated by insecurities that I was a poor provider and as a man, I should be able to keep my wife's purse full. In my imagination, I would create comparison stories about other marriages. I compared myself to those perfect husbands who provided their wives with much larger homes and an unlimited checking account. And even though I made multiples of what my father ever made, I still carried the "broke" mentality I had developed from his examples.

So I let her criticism of our financial state trigger me. I made a pretty good salary, but we spent every dollar every month. I let myself get offended by her criticism. Sure, there was an element of truth in her criticism but combined with a bad Me story, her remarks triggered me terribly.

My anger at my tools, computers, and other inanimate objects is an incompetence story I tell myself. The complexity of the world feeds this story. There is no way I can be as competent as a computer technician, yet I trigger myself when something goes wrong. In the case of our frustration we face dealing with the complexity of the world, forgiveness of self is the only recourse.

As I consider growing up with my siblings, a couple of Me stories pop into my mind. Since I was the firstborn, in one story I'm the center of the universe, and my siblings should respect me. A second important Me story was the idea that I abandoned people. I left every girlfriend in college without warning or long breakups. I left my first marriage quite suddenly without any advance discussion. This is where my siblings' accusation stung me because there was truth to it, even though I denied it.

But the Me story at the root of much of my behavior and triggers was with the story I had about the woman next door who branded me as homely. To deal with the intense personal attacks about my looks, I had built an emotional wall to protect myself. I moved on quickly from relationships to avoid getting too attached and vulnerable. I told myself that women were cruel and heartless and didn't deserve consideration.

What is the other side of your current story?

Who or what was the "other" you wrote down in the first question of the clarification section? Who has triggered you? Can you see, hear, and feel that other person's point of view? Try to use all three senses to elucidate their story. When we are able to see the other person's perspective, we are able to focus on the elements of truth in what we heard that triggered us.

One of our first reactions to a trigger involving another person is to "prove" we are right. Let's assume the other person might know something you don't know. What are some possible truths that may have elicited their action that then triggered you?

Maybe we thought they were doing something to intentionally hurt us when in reality they were caught in their own Me story and not even thinking of us at all. Whether you are right or wrong, dwelling on the other person won't help you learn about yourself. The small satisfaction of believing ourselves to be "right" can actually hurt our personal growth.

The story of the man thinking about his boat motor at the beginning of this section illustrates this concept perfectly. Other people are ensconced in their own little world, thinking as much about themselves as you are about yourself.

My siblings' feelings of being abandoned by me are definitely valid. I could see their point of view. Generally, my siblings are quite close to each other. I am the most distant by far. When I left college, I moved a two-day drive away from home. I married a woman who did not like to be near my family. Was this intentional or subconscious?

And the fact that they held on to that resentment for fifty years tells me that they must have suffered greatly. I had never heard that story before. Why would they bring that up after so many years? When someone holds a story for that long, they must have a message for us.

3. Transformation

The purpose of all this work is to help you to transform yourself so you will grow. We can only reach our goals if we change enough to become the person we need to be. If I'm in debt and living paycheck to paycheck and get triggered about money, I need to change. For most people that means becoming sick and tired of being sick and tired of money issues. Since it's better to work on your personal growth before a crisis hits, I wanted to focus on goals and purpose before we discussed triggers.

Transformation will come when we realize that freedom from triggers is not an external problem. There is no problem outside of us. We will know we have found the truth when we are no longer triggered.

What results do you want to produce?

In this step, we work backward. Instead of thinking of the story first, we need to decide what results we want in our life and how our current story produced a set of results. By now you should be aware that there is more than one side to every situation and not just looking at life, other people's actions and your reactions, through your own set of beliefs.

Someone once said, "Insanity is doing the same thing over and over but expecting different results." Many people attribute this to Einstein. No matter who said it, we know from observation the truth of this statement.

The results you want out of any given situation could be numerous and diverse. There's probably an emotional component. What story would you really like to tell about the event that triggered you? What feelings would you like to have if the event occurred again? What actions would you like to take if the event happened again? What outcome would you like for yourself and others? Maybe you want to be relaxed or confident instead of angry or stressed. Maybe there's a spiritual component, a social piece, or a physical element. This vision comes out of our frontal cortex and requires rational thinking.

Maybe our protagonist would have liked to have had harmony and love at home, probably more satisfaction and profit from his business, and finally, be at peace with living in his town. Or maybe he wanted to ditch everything and go overseas or go to college and fulfill his dream of becoming an architect.

Don't think in terms of wrong or right answers. Think in terms of what results you want to produce in your life. Do not judge your desires based on old stories. In Part V I discuss old tribal frames that may block us from achieving certain results.

As you answer these questions, don't be afraid to go down rabbit holes to examine your beliefs and stories that are at the root of what triggered you. We can get pretty deep into our personal psychology if we take the time, are honest with ourselves, and reflective.

Thinking about my story of abandoning people led me to examine that aspect of my personality. On the one hand, I do leave people without long goodbyes or emotional drama. On the other hand, this trait has been an advantage during times of loss. I lost a brother suddenly during the same week the 9/11 attack occurred.

I lost four young children I had adopted from Russia. Although I was their father only a short time, losing a child is one of any parents' worst nightmares. I was emotionally attached to them. When I relinquished the children to a new home, I could have been devastated. I was able to let them go with the hope that they would find a better home and not mourn for weeks or months.

I guess you could say I'm not that emotional. I certainly have feelings, but I don't let my emotions control me. I see emotion as just a door you pass through to get to the place you want to be. This protects me emotionally from loss and allows me to move on quickly. Many people get stuck in sadness and grief with losses. I never have. I see this as a gift from my neighbor. On the other hand, this has limited my emotional connection to people. I'm often seen as cold.

There are always trade-offs in life. You have to decide what trade-offs you want to make. Every decision excludes other possible paths. You may judge a path right for you that others criticize you for. Part of the path to growth is to disregard other people's opinions. Sure you can see if their knowledge is useful to you, but in the end, it is your story and your life.

Which story would you like for your life?

You may think, "Duh, the ideal story of course!" But, not so fast! This is often where people get stuck. They have an ideal story but deep down may feel unworthy of creating a better outcome and instead choose to continue with their Me story.

For example, you may desire to have a great marriage with your spouse. Yet you feel unworthy of their love and so continue the self-defeating Me stories to *prove* you are unloved. You may desire to make lots of money but feel guilty about having more than others. So you sabotage yourself by choosing the Me stories to *prove* people with money are bad. Or you may desire better sexual experiences but are held back by tribal mores that block you.

In Part V I discuss larger meta-stories that may be holding us back. These are usually tribal stories that we buy into subconsciously. We tend to surround ourselves with people who have similar meta-stories, which perpetuates our own story.

The hardest part of this exercise is releasing your Me story. For most of your life, you have used your Me stories to validate your view of life. Maybe you have also used it to escape responsibility for owning your situation in life, whatever that is. The key here is to be totally honest with yourself. No one is going to judge your answer except you!

For my Me story, I had to acknowledge that I left people and even though I am not responsible for their feelings, I played a role in their feeling abandoned. My father used to admonish me, "Stop crying or I'll give you something to cry about." Is my behavior some protective measure to shield my own emotions or just the training from my dad? I do cry a lot but for other people's pain not my own.

I decided to examine this aspect of my personality in more depth to understand it and determine if I want to make any changes. Am I contributing to the evil in the world by harming others by being emotionally detached? It's sad but true.

Going forward I have resolved to mitigate this type of behavior in myself.

What is the revelation, insight, or lesson you learned from this process?

This is the "Y" branch question in this process—the fork in the road. How you answer this question forms the crux of where you will go from here. This is the kind of feedback we need in order to change.

As I discussed in Chapter 10, whenever something happens and we go through the story, feelings, action, result cycle, we reach a decision point. We can either dismiss the whole sequence, not learn a thing and accept that pattern of living as our fate—and the next time a trigger occurs, we go through the same cycle. Or we can assess what just happened, see what we can learn and move one step closer to being the kind of person we want to be and living the life we want to live.

In either case, our brain will receive feedback. In the first instance, we reinforce negative feedback creating a downward plunge. In the second path, we generate positive feedback, which will create exponential growth of our competence and subsequently to our goals.

I took away two insights from this exercise. First, I discovered my inclination to move on quickly from others is linked to the stories I told myself after being taunted about my looks. Women were cruel and attaching to them was very risky. My second insight was that we are so deeply interconnected with people that actions I took fifty years ago are still resonating in the universe. This has profound implications for the choices I make going forward.

4. Redirection

By now we have explored our triggers and why we get triggered. Hopefully, you have achieved some insight that will transform your character. Now it's time to set a new path for ourselves. Pointing ourselves in a new direction will give us hope that a solution can be found to your problems.

What new story has ensued from the previous work?

When we gain new information about ourselves, this revelation is actually a new story. We might realize we are more competent than we were seconds ago. We may find we are more grateful for our past experiences. We may find we no longer value old goals and now have a new purpose.

What feelings are you having about what you have learned?

A new story creates new feelings! The work you have to do here is to reinforce the idea that every emotion is coming from a story.

My new story is that I need to understand my actions have long-term and wide-reaching effects. The effect my neighbor had on my life was significant. All of the women I have interacted with bear the brunt of the stories I created around her characterization of me. What effect did leaving home have on my siblings' life? Did they make relationship decisions based on how I acted? It was a large butterfly effect indeed.

Should I feel regret for my past actions? I think regret is a wasted emotion and rarely spend time on it. I am not living in the past. My feelings are more akin to Peter Parker's (Spiderman) philosophy: With great power comes great responsibility. When we realize how significant our impact on others is, it is a humbling experience, not one of regret.

What actions will you take based on these new feelings?

Here is where we see if we really analyzed our story properly. If the actions will not lead to the results we want, then something is missing from our examination of the facts.

When I discovered how my siblings felt after all those years, I had feelings of sympathy. I cannot change the past, but I can change the meaning of what I remember. One response I can work on is being present when others trigger me. Being able to listen without reacting is a powerful tool for me to develop. Social media, for all its bad qualities, is a proving ground for this. I used to spend time arguing with others who represented opposite viewpoints. Now, I practice letting those posts flow by and watching my inner reaction.

I also have had to consider how I think about that neighbor and my stories about women. Are all women cruel? Does my neighbor deserve forgiveness for what she did to me?

If your old story resurfaces what will you do to break this roadblock?

One of our most important superpowers is that we alone decide how the memories of our past affect us. Those who control the present, control the past, but nothing says we have to succumb to our old interpretations of the past or even which aspects of past events we choose to remember.

You assigned meaning to your past, and you can change that meaning. The past event may or may not have occurred. We hallucinate events often, but you control the present by creating the story you want about the past.

Once you control how you interpret your memories, then you control the present, which controls your future.

Many people get stuck on how they interpret events that happened in the past. They spend years with a psychologist trying to "come to terms" with some particular event. They stay stuck, though, when they continue to see themselves as a victim of said event and don't learn to redefine the past.

Reinterpreting how we think about the past is just as valuable as being able to change the past!

In fact, it may be more valuable since it reveals to us how powerful we actually are. That we can stop playing a victim. The switch from seeing ourselves as a victim to seeing ourselves as powerful can take years when we refuse to let go of our old stories and stay stuck in victim stories. Or it can take a millisecond. By letting those old stories go and crafting new ones, we become powerful instantly. Learning to examine our lives with this process is very therapeutic. Examining childhood memories that triggered us can expose how our stories originated.

If you feel scared or threatened by this information or reject it outright, it could be a story you created. Our brain wants to remain on standby and prefers to avoid the work required to be totally responsible for our life.

I've spoken with people who cling to past memories even though those memories are hurting them now. It appeared to me that their difficulty in letting the old memories go had to do with losing their identity as a victim. But that is only mind reading on my part!

When we are totally responsible for something (our life circumstances), our amygdala creates lots of fear. New responsibility involves unknowable unknowns (chaos) and that means potential danger.

When our first child arrived, I was afraid. At that time I had taken responsibility for school and work projects, and I had taken care of my younger siblings. When babysitting, my level of responsibility had been pretty high, but I had my parents to fall back on. The stakes for those tasks were not as high as being completely responsible for a helpless infant.

We adopted our first child from Texas and drove home to West Virginia. I remember trembling while driving I was so terrified of my new role as a father. Knowing I had total responsibility for this new completely helpless life was very scary. Accepting the responsibility and watching my children grow has been my most rewarding life experience, albeit one of seemingly never-ending chaos!

5. Incentivization

The last step in a good system is creating a good reason to keep doing it. What is the most powerful mechanism we have for motivating our behavior? Dopamine. It's the neurotransmitter we need to survive. Social media companies have figured out how to activate our dopamine response, and make a lot of money doing it. It's time we do the same for ourselves.

We are always incentivizing ourselves. The normal path is to reward that which feels good. Instead, we should reward that which produces the best long-term results. For example, we would much rather lie in bed eating potato chips then get up and exercise. Therefore, we need to create a way to make the latter activity more pleasurable. By focusing on the long-term benefit we are able to reach the destination we really desire.

Create dopamine hits that move you to where you want to go.

Psychology professor and best-selling author Robert Cialdini writes about how human brains crave commitment and consistency. When you are trying to create a new habit this is a tough barrier to overcome. Our brain wants to continue with the old ways despite a desire for a new outcome.

The way over this hurdle is to consistently take small steps and reward yourself with something that gives you a dopamine hit. For me, it's dark chocolate. While writing this book I work for three hours then reward myself with a piece of chocolate. I won't eat chocolate unless I have done the work that day. Find what pleasurable reward you can give yourself. Maybe you enjoy a fancy coffee at Starbucks, maybe an exhilarating hike in the woods or using social media.

Understanding what makes you tick is the key. Each of us has a different trigger for dopamine. Food, attention, sex, validation, exercise, and drugs all release dopamine. It's important that we don't let rewards create long-term detriments. There are two critical ways this can happen. First, don't set your goal for a reward too high. If you struggle to make one sales call and set a goal to do thirty in a day, this won't work. Start out by rewarding yourself for one call. Then double the goal before you give yourself the second reward and so on. Second, don't give in halfway to your goal. Recall that our brains are pattern-recognizing machines and need repetition, so self-discipline is required before automatic responses take over.

The process of doing new activities creates new stories in our brain about our competence. This increases our confidence in the feedback loops. Every success breeds more success. Eventually, you've climbed the 80/20 curve to become one of the best in your field.

If you are starting to panic at the thought of facing the chaos of the unknown, don't worry. This is a normal response to chaos. Embracing it and forcing personal growth will set you free. In Part VI I explore why you should embrace chaos and how to do it in the best way.

When you embrace a balance between stability and chaos, you will find a new zest for life.

Next Steps

Need more help understanding and implementing the Debugging Software? Go to rebootmystories.com for more in depth explanation of this tool and how to create systems to motivate you to reach your goals.

PART IV
OPERATING SYSTEM BUGS

There was an old man standing by the side of the road leading to a small town. People would stop and ask the man, "What kind of people live in the town?"

The man would reply, "What kind of people lived in the town where you came from?" If they answered, "The town was full of thieves and liars," the old man would say, "Well, this town has the same kind of people—thieves and liars."

If the stranger answered, "Very kind and honest people lived in my previous town," then the old man would say, "The folks in this town are just like that too."

The old man was right in both cases.

15

FAULTY CODE OVERWRITING: MIND READING

Just like our computer, our brain gets crowded with garbage data, programming viruses, and random noise. When we go through the Debugging Software, glitches that create confirmation biases and prevent clear thinking may trip us up.

Trying to separate what is true from nonsense is a task we will undertake in this part. You may look over the topics in this section and think that they do not apply to you. I'll bet that everyone reading here has experienced most, if not all, of these bugs. Maybe we feel we are only a little bit addicted to social media, for example. But if it is distracting us from our goals or keeping us from facing certain realities, then it's likely we are infected.

One defective pattern of our programming language is the desire of our software code to want to overwrite reality.

Our brains have a bug that was created in prehistoric times when negotiating with people was a life or death activity. This bug involves reading the minds of our fellow humans. We love to infer what people are thinking from a phrase they speak, a look they give, or how they cross their arms. This is part of the brain's energy management and threat deterrence systems. It is much easier to pretend we know what someone is thinking than to engage with him or her and risk a conflict.

In modern times, our mind reading has changed from worrying about threats to worrying about status. We worry about what other people are thinking of us. No doubt, they are thinking badly of us. At least we tell ourselves that story. Our amygdala is programmed to view all actions as threats and react with a fight, flight, fawn, or freeze response. A person thinking poorly about us threatens our social status.

What we are really doing when we try to read people's minds is actually projecting our thoughts, fears, and inner turmoil onto them. Our confirmation biases trick us into believing that other people see the world exactly as we do. As part of our egocentric view of the world, we think that since we are thinking about ourselves all the time, then other people must be thinking of us too. However, the people we think are thinking of us are just as self-absorbed as we are. They're afraid we're thinking badly of them. As a consequence, each of us feels offended by the actions others take because we can only envision them taking such actions to attack us in some manner.

In other words, we are triggered by our own thoughts about what others are thinking! Like the travelers in the previous tale going to a new town, we are projecting our inner beliefs onto others and triggering ourselves.

People often cite money as the main source of conflict in a relationship, but I believe it is probably mind reading. When entering a relationship we have expectations about how the other person will treat us, how they feel about sex, money, children, and so on. In truth, those expectations are largely the result of projecting our internal stories onto the other person. We use mind-reading exercises rather than discussions.

Besides being egocentric and believing others are thinking about us, many of us put together a plotline where they are actually oppressing us. The primary virus infecting our code is the inclination to create victim stories about ourselves. This defective code will work hard to construct a story that another's actions are designed to oppress or hurt us.

Today, it's unlikely that the people we encounter are going to put poison in our food or a knife in our back, and the threats are mostly imagined. Except for the occasional psychopath, people are not walking around thinking about how to hurt us; they are too consumed in their own world.

In sum, mind reading is a dangerous game we play that at best protects us from minor threats and at worst destroys relationships with others. Fortunately, we have not yet reached the point where technology, much fewer people, can read our minds.

If you catch yourself injecting what someone else is thinking into your story, then stop. Trace the thoughts back to your own Me stories. That is where these mind-reading tricks are originating.

Psychological projection is very easy to see in other people but challenging to see in ourselves. Gossip is a popular pastime of the mind readers. Sitting at a table with gossipers can give you an insight into where each person has Me stories as they broadcast their inner psyches. For example, the Facebook story of the wife worried about their relationship ending while her husband was preoccupied with a motorboat problem is a common projection of insecurity.

In the 1980s I ran for and won a political office in West Virginia. Without fail every time I talked to the press I found a different story in the paper or on TV about what I said. I learned to talk without saying anything, and the press would read my mind and print a story exposing their biases. In the beginning, I used to be angry about what the journalists wrote but later got a laugh reading it. I now understand they were engaged in mind reading to suit their own agenda.

In our Debugging Software analysis of our trigger, we need to figure out if we are mind reading or have real facts. If you determine you were mind reading, go deep into your Me story analysis. It's likely your perception of another's thoughts is a projection of your own inner fears, anger or despair.

16

IMPROPER HARDWARE ACCELERATION: ADDICTION STORIES

When we process an event without learning anything from it, we reinforce the negative outcome of that event and create a negative feedback loop. One of the more common results of negative feedback loops is the addiction story. This is where, in the face of continued failure to address our problems, we look to substances to distract us and numb the pain of our failures.

Addiction is reinforcing the feedback loop in our programming language and exponentially escalates bad outcomes.

Some people try to be the savior of the world. They attempt to legislate everything as a way to control people and impose more order on society. These people seek to ban addictive substances. However, the "saviors" fail to realize their demand is an infinite supply of substances or activities that trigger a release of dopamine. People use alcohol, drugs, sex, food, video games, social media, and an infinite number of other means of escape from having to examine their current life story they created.

Banning the next substance or game or porn site does not stop the behavior any more than banning prostitution has stopped the sale of sex. The dopamine rush that occurs when we engage in addictive behaviors makes it rewarding to continue. The saviors would need to find a way to stop dopamine releases to solve this problem.

When all else fails we become addicted to our work rather than face our problems. Feeling that the office can't function without us gives us the sense that we are too important to face those personal issues.

Humans will usually rather hide behind addictive behavior than face the truth about themselves. Social media makes it very easy to adopt addictive behavior that distracts us from our problems.

When the addiction causes physical harm, the person blames himself or herself and even turns to self-destruction. The hazard here is that people in strong addiction stories build their cocoon with layers of lies. They play the victim game by surrounding themselves with enablers who make excuses for them.

Jack Kent wrote the children's book *There's No Such Thing As A Dragon*. In the story, little Billy finds a dragon in his bedroom one morning. When he tells his mother about the dragon, she says, "There is no such thing as a dragon". As the mother continues to ignore the dragon it grows to the point where it fills the entire house. The mother tries to conduct normal activities while ignoring this giant dragon in an amusing way. Only at the end of the story, when the parents acknowledge that the dragon exists, does the dragon shrink.

Of course, that book is really written for adults who refuse to acknowledge the mess they are in. The "dragons" are those problems we ignore. The longer you ignore problems, the bigger they get. Ignored problems grow until they encompass all the people in your world, not just you.

People that mask their problems are only deceiving themselves. And even though their lives appear in order, the opposite is true. There are areas of their lives that make them uncomfortable and they are afraid to confront. Their brain is trying to make a pattern out of the chaos in order to conserve energy. The addiction is familiar and even comfortable. Their brain fears the alternative story—the truth—because that is the unknown.

Addictions create the worst negative feedback loops and must be confronted with truth. Unless it is a tiger chasing us, running away from pain is worse than the pain itself.

It is said that addicts usually don't change until they hit rock bottom. This is where they confront the results of their lies and finally get unbearably uncomfortable. Unfortunately, neither you nor I can save them—they have to save themselves.

I started smoking cigarettes in college. The problem I was trying to ignore was interacting with women. I was trying to play the cool guy everyone liked. But in my senior year of college, I contracted a severe case of bronchitis, which sidelined me for a couple of months. In my case, that was enough of a bottom to quit smoking. It also helped that none of the group of friends I developed in college smoked. Coincidence?

It may be sad when someone we love is caught in an addiction story. The best thing we can do for them is to evaluate whether we are enabling their behavior by accepting the lies they tell. Seeing others as victims often leads us to believe that they are incapable of overcoming their situation and so we develop enabling behaviors towards them.

Addicts require enablers.

You may be thinking that homeless addicts and Twitter users don't have enablers. That would be wrong. Facebook, Twitter, Instagram, and YouTube are tremendous enablers. We get a dopamine hit every time someone likes the content we post. Video games use the same mechanism to lure us. City and state governments are enablers. They provide the homeless with free needles and allow them to break laws by defecating in the streets. Like individuals, tribal groups engage in uniform behavior by signaling their virtue. They seek recognition and hope to prove their superiority. Homeless camps are evidence of mass enabling by a societal tribe that is blinded by its need to feel compassionate superiority.

If you are an enabler, ask yourself what payoff you are getting. Does it make you feel important? Do you feel superior to the addicts? Or does it make you feel needed (a substitute for love)?

For the huge social media and gaming companies, the payoff is massive profits and social influence. The CEOs of these companies get to feel very important. Maybe they even feel superior.

Russian novelist Fyodor Dostoyevsky had some of the deepest insight into human behavior in his novel *The Brothers Karamazov*:

"Above all, don't lie to yourself. The man who lies to himself and listens to his own lie comes to a point that he cannot distinguish the truth within him, or around him, and so loses all respect for himself and for others. And having no respect he ceases to love."

There is profound wisdom in this quote. When we lie to ourselves we cannot love ourselves because we lose respect for ourselves. When we do not love ourselves, we cannot love others.

Do addicts love themselves? Probably not. Addiction is all about deceiving oneself. Breaking the chains of addiction requires one to always tell the truth about their situation.

And if you think you do not lie to yourself, consider your confirmation bias is a huge deception you swim in every minute of every day. You cannot escape it. We all lie to ourselves. Breaking that cycle requires some deep time in the debugger.

17

MESSY CODE: DRAMA QUEENS AND TOXIC PEOPLE

WHEN WRITING COMPUTER code, the skill of the coder plays a role in how efficient the software program executes. What a skillful coder might do in one hundred lines of code, a less experienced person might need one thousand lines. The poor code may create all kinds of branches that go awry from the results desired. In the end, the less skillful coder might create software that has lots of bugs, takes much longer to run, and gives erroneous results.

Likewise, many times we encounter melodramatic or toxic people in our life. These people have stories that are full of drama and shout out "I'm a victim." They maintain stories where everything seems to go wrong for them all the time. They jump from crisis to crisis and are always looking for someone to save them.

Toxic people's stories are messy code that breaks our programming. It detours us down paths away from where we need to go for growth.

Some books suggest we should rid toxic people from our lives because they drag us down. This is definitely a good practice.

Like addicts, we cannot save people who always create drama in their lives.

Drama queens and toxic people need others to validate them. They are using great drama so people pay attention to them, and they need enablers to watch the show—just like addicts.

If we find that our life is full of toxic people or we continually find ourselves in a relationship with a toxic person, then a Me story is at play. Why are we performing in their show or clapping in their audience validating their performances?

It's not the other person.

Maybe we have a strong desire to be a savior. We crave the love or recognition we might receive. Remember, people seek those things due to a childhood story.

Maybe the drama is something we enjoy. Many people create a story that their life is boring and are attracted to all the excitement of a toxic person or drama queen. If we enjoy being around a drama queen, have we given up control of our own story? It's worth examining our stories to see what is at play. It's not an accident that we are constantly around these types of people.

Owning rental houses exposed me to lots of drama queen stories. I had the police call me when tenants were found running outside the building naked in the middle of the night and had to chase bats out of apartments when a tenant freaked out at two in the morning.

One of the houses I owned had been subdivided into side-by-side apartments. Two young gay men rented these. One kept his place spotless. He was always painting and decorating it. In the other apartment, the tenant was a slob. Dirty clothing was strewn everywhere and dirty dishes littered the apartment. There were so many cockroaches that I had to fumigate the house every week for three months to clean it up. The tidy tenant's life was as orderly as his apartment. Likewise, the second tenant's life was as messy as his apartment—full of drama. He was often in bar fights and would end up in the hospital from stab wounds or some other trauma. At one point he nearly died. Yet the two men were best friends. Each seemed attracted to the other's story. One life was full of order, the other chaos. It was a very toxic relationship for the man who prided himself in order and beauty.

In most of the Western world, there is no physical reason to remain in a toxic relationship. Our brains, however, often confuse safety with the known over the unknown. So people end up staying in an abusive relationship because of psychological reasons. If your spouse is abusing you but you feel you can't leave the safety of the income and home, what storyline are you telling yourself? Often times, the fear of a loss of social status overrides our actual abuse too.

If you find that your life is full of drama or toxic people, go through the Debugging Software. Figure out what story is at play when a trigger happens and what fears you are failing to address.

Remember that if someone is lying to you, they have been lying to themselves for much longer.

18

MEMORY INTENSIVE PROGRAMMING: HALLUCINATIONS, FANTASY STORIES, AND SELF-DELUSION

AFTER READING ABOUT the power we have to create stories, you may be thinking you can create any story you want. That's almost true but not quite.

There is this New Age fad of believing you can speak things into existence by just thinking the right thoughts or repeating the right mantras over and over. The creed is that your dreams will manifest or materialize out of nothing. Deepak Chopra and Wayne Dyer have famously promoted this viewpoint. I think we must obey the laws of physics and mathematics. Although we probably can conquer death with science, meditating did not make Dyer immortal.

I suppose we could be living in *The Matrix* (a movie I enjoyed) or *The Holographic Universe* (a book I enjoyed) or maybe there are multiverses, and all possible results exist simultaneously. It's even possible that the world came into existence through a divine Creator who will rescue us from our mischief. But no matter which of these possibilities we embrace, we have to work within certain laws. We cannot jump off a building and expect to fly without some extraneous help. Even in a simulation, the mathematical code limits us.

There is no clear evidence that meditation alone will manifest our dreams out of nothing. I have not seen pictures of food fall from the heavens as Buddhist monks in Tibet meditate. Someone still has to till the ground, plant the food, and water it.

We don't attract money like manna from heaven. When we create a story, *that* opens our mind to new possibilities. Opportunities that were always around us, but we ignored may seem like a manifestation when they appear now. However, that is due to our increased awareness.

Occasionally someone will claim they meditated about money and suddenly found a hundred dollar bill on the street as "proof." This happens when we buy a new car and suddenly see the same car everywhere we drive. It's an awareness phenomenon, not a manifestation.

A religious man was trapped on the roof of his house during a flood. Three times rescuers came by in boats to save him. Each time he told them to go away, that God was going to save him. He drowned and upon reaching heaven asked God why He didn't save him from the flood. God replied, "I sent three boats to rescue you. I can't help someone living in a fantasy."

It's important to stay grounded in reality when using the Debugging Software to create our desired stories. When our story is disconnected from the reality we are hallucinating. We cannot break the laws of physics.

There is a fine line between someone who visualizes what they want (i.e., creates a story), takes action to get it, and uses the 80/20 Principle to make it happen versus someone who hallucinates.

Self-help guru Napoleon Hill wrote a book called *Think and Grow Rich,* but the essence of his book is that once you think right, you have to take action. He does not say that thinking will manifest things. Hill was exposed to the wealthy, and he changed his story and created his own wealth. When you are thinking right, you see opportunities and act on them. We are all exposed to many opportunities, but most of the time we have the wrong mindset and don't act.

Surprisingly, large numbers of people go through life hallucinating without ever touching magic mushrooms or LSD. Many people are attracted to misinformation and conspiracy theories and are totally disconnected from any reality.

I recently read of a young journalist who used the word *hampster* in a news article. Her editor carefully explained that the correct spelling of the word was *hamster.* The young woman said she had spelled the word with a *P* since she was young, and therefore it must be the correct spelling!

After her boss left, the woman called her mother and, while on the speakerphone so the whole office could hear, complained about how mean her boss was. Instead of correcting her, her mother told her to speak to her boss's supervisor and complain! It is the perfect example of two people sharing and reinforcing each other's self-delusions!

If the story we are telling ourselves is leading us down a path where life is falling apart and our actions lead to catastrophes, it's time to change. We sometimes need someone to help correct this bug, someone outside our tribe.

If, on the other hand, sad and toxic people are telling you that you are living in a fantasy world while your life is going great, the story is serving you well. In the words of Denzel Washington, "When people don't like you, it's because your spirit enrages their demons." Those who want to play the victim are always attacking successful people.

The bottom line is that we can tell what reality is by looking at the results our story produces. If we get fired from our journalism job because we refuse to spell *hamster* correctly, then be honest about the results. Don't blame the editor for your hallucination.

Now there is one caveat to this. Our minds have far more power over us than we are aware. There is something in medical science called the placebo effect. When people receive a sugar pill in a drug trial approximately 30 percent to 40 percent will be cured. All people in the trial are told the medicine may cure their condition, but the half receiving the sugar pill experience a self-hypnosis phenomenon. People who are cured of disease after prayer are also experiencing this phenomenon—even non-believers! Self-hypnosis does not change the world but it does change how you perceive it. The brain can biochemically alter the body. Meditating Buddhist monks are able to change blood pressure and heart rate with their minds during meditation.

As I mentioned previously, some people who create a mantra of "I am" statements do succeed at creating the results. Looking at a large sample of people who do this, only 30 to 40 percent, the same number who experience the placebo effect, are successful.

If you are capable of self-hypnosis, then give it a shot. You won't be able to drop money from the sky or fly without an aircraft, but maybe you can convince yourself you are capable of success, just like the con man who got the engineering job at DuPont which I describe in Chapter 33.

19

SECONDARY VIRUSES: CULTS AND CONSPIRACY THEORY GROUP STORIES

"Instead of protesting and trying to change the world, first win the war of evil within yourself. To make the world a better place, first do the things you have to do every day. And do them; do them every day"

—Jordan Peterson

WHEN A VIRUS infects the software on our computer, it seeks to take control of our operating system. Sometimes a virus will delete all our old data and erase the system history. When a mental virus infects our brain, it can alter our perceptions and force us into negative Me stories.

When infected with such mental viruses we search for those who are likewise infected. By reinforcing our stories the virus grows in power over us. Maybe, this is part of our brain's energy conservation strategy. However, sometimes we get absorbed into another tribal group's identity. We assume all their beliefs as if infected with a virus that erases all our data (i.e., memories).

It's especially easy to catch these mental viruses when we see ourselves as victims and align ourselves with a group that promises to save us from some real or imagined oppressor. These groups often teach us that people outside the group are sheep being led astray. We give up our individual beliefs and submissively align with the leader or groupthink to the exclusion of reality

Conspiracy-focused chat groups on the internet draw people in who believe they are victims of Big Pharma or the Military-Industrial Complex or the Illuminati.

Charismatic leaders attract many people with low self-esteem. Religious leaders or utopianists attract those who seek to be "saved."

People with little confidence seem to buy into other people's stories rather than creating their own. Those with low confidence are susceptible to charlatans. People who buy into conspiracy theories or join a cult have one commonality: they feel powerless. Let's look at these conspiracies and cults for a moment.

People who fall prey to cults often create wild theories that Big Pharm or oil companies are conspiring to harm them. As far as large companies or organizations conspiring to oppress you, I doubt that. I worked in a very large chemical corporation that owned a large oil company and a large pharmaceutical company.

Sometimes the role of profits gets warped in an organization and bad outcomes occur. But this is due to human failing where self-interest goes awry, not grand conspiracies. The problem-solving principle called Occam's razor states that the simplest explanation for any observation is the most likely. Humans act in their own self-interest. Employees in big pharmaceutical companies are not sitting in their cubicles trying to figure out how to poison you with their vaccines.

Incompetence is also at play. There is something called the

Peter Principle that postulates that people in a corporation rise to their level of incompetence. That is, once they reach a level in the company where they are no longer competent, then they stop being promoted. Large companies have thousands of middle managers who are hopelessly incompetent.

One time years ago, I was in my research lab laughing my butt off at a *Dilbert* cartoon. A high-level manager walked by. When he saw why I was laughing, he shouted, "That's not funny!" The truth triggered him. The reason why Scott Adams's comic strip has endured for so many decades is the fundamental truth of management's incompetence.

So if a corporation or government bureaucracy does something wrong, the most likely explanations are incompetence or self-interest gone awry, not a grand conspiracy.

Believing in conspiracy theories takes your power away. It won't help you achieve any of your life's goals.

∽

One way to determine if you are in a cult is to question the tenets of the group or try to introduce new ideas. If members continue to interact with you civilly, it's probably not a cult. If they declare you a heretic or a denier or apostate and refuse to interact with you, then run away. They are seeking to control you not help you.

When we are members of a group of like-minded people, working through the Debugging Software can give us insights as to why we belong to that group. We have to decide if it is what we really want.

I'm not saying that believing in a creator means you're in a cult. I actually think a belief in something greater is a net positive as I discuss in Chapter 26—as long as you don't evangelize your beliefs—religious or not. Groups that believe their way is the only way broadcast their insecurity. Religious groups are all certain that theirs is the only path as are pseudo-religious groups espousing environmental or animal rights. I want to be persuaded of a belief by my own volition not by being manipulated into feeling afraid that hell fires await me for not believing. How an organization attempts to persuade others depends on the story they have created about their beliefs.

Cult-like groups are viruses because anytime they create in their flock stories of being powerless or victims that produces bad outcomes they are hurting their followers. Cults expect you to give up control of your personal stories and adopt without question the group story. This is about who has the power in a relationship—you or the group leaders.

Followers in cult-like groups have one set of stories while the leaders operate to a different beat. Many religious and social justice activist leaders spend considerable effort proselytizing the masses. This comes out of the strong need for order. If you engage in this type of behavior please recognize that treating others as needing your "correct" viewpoint is a form of tyranny. Whether it is Stalin or Joe the evangelist, it is evil behavior. This is an example of Dostoyevsky's axiom that we all contribute to the evil in the world.

When our story makes us think we are better than others, it is a bad story because it causes us to view other human beings as incapable of doing the "right" thing per our values, and thus powerless. People who become evangelists for anything have taken their confirmation bias to another level. True believers have one way to see the world and are not open to alternatives.

The short-term result may seem good for us, but the long-term result for society is bad. Tyrant's attempts to control the people have always led to death and suffering. Creating a world that is full of suffering returns fear and hate back toward us. The Roman Catholic Medieval Inquisition was responsible for the murder of many apostates in the twelfth century. Islam and communism have had tendencies to create periods of large-scale killing as well.

At times when murderous tendencies occur any organization can devolve into a cult-like atmosphere. It was not just Jim Jones. All the people that followed these groups believed their creed was the only path to salvation.

People who believe they know best tend to try to control others in order to make the world safer. Years ago, when I was babysitting, I acted as a dictator in an attempt to feel safe. When we try to create order through force, we broadcast that we are afraid. Trying to gain power by oppressing others exposes weakness. People who act in this way do not have their act together. Remember, people are projecting their internal thoughts and beliefs. That is why we read stories of ministers who tell their flock to abstain from sex and are caught with prostitutes. Or social justice activists who want the world to change but live in their mom's basement.

As Dr. Jordan Peterson so clearly proclaimed, "If you want to save the world, first clean your room." People who gain personal competence from having their own lives in order are much more capable of making lasting change in the world than those who don't.

If you believe in some purpose for your life, then work on being a better person first. As I've discussed in Chapter 11, use the feedback loops to grow so that you can work on solutions for that purpose. Don't try to impose your will on others. When you have developed adequate competence, your effect on the world will be far more positive.

20
POOR LOGGING
METHODOLOGY:
DEPRESSION, DESPAIR AND
COMPARISON STORIES

―――――――――――

WHEN PROBLEMS OCCUR during software execution a log file records the events. Often these occur when the system is overwhelmed.

Everyone has had moments in their life when they have felt overwhelmed and depressed about their circumstances. Life is full of suffering and pain and in the end, we all die. Nothing could be more depressing than that.

There are undoubtedly people with chemical brain imbalances that cause depressive states. There is a feedback loop between body and mind that is also at play. Scientists now understand that our thoughts influence our biochemistry and our biochemistry influences our thoughts. Diet also plays a crucial role in our brain health as I discuss in Chapter 30. Doctors, however, too often prescribe and patients submissively accept the extensive use of anti-depressants. Anti-depressants really don't solve the root problem for those with normal brain function. The drugs just mask the symptoms.

The root problem is the log file you are creating when one of these catastrophic events occurs. People create a story of helplessness and self-pity and store that pattern in their log file. The perceived powerlessness reinforces their view of themselves being a victim.

When we perceive something bad happening to us, and we create a story that generates sad emotions, what are the actions created by that grief? For some people, grief leads to an addiction to hide the pain. Others turn their sad stories into a reason to craft a new purpose in life. Without a new purpose, our grief can lead to a negative feedback loop. Most depression has its origin in this negative feedback loop.

Think about death, for example. We all feel sad when someone we love dies. What is really happening though? The deceased is no longer in pain and does not hear our wails of sorrow. We are sad for ourselves. Sadness over the death of a loved one can create self-pity or fear of our own mortality or anger. It depends on the story you are telling yourself about the death.

When we have a healthy perspective on death, we will not reinforce our story with more negative thoughts. We can be glad the deceased is no longer suffering and remember the joyful experiences we shared. We can take the time to reevaluate our life and decide whether or not we are living it to the fullest or wasting time on social media. Remember you are choosing what meaning to assign to events. There are all kinds of meanings we can attach to our memories of a loved one that provide better results and keep us from getting stuck.

Another rut we get stuck in that feeds depressing thoughts is our comparison stories. Comparison stories are a double-edged sword. We often want to compare ourselves with others. And we tend to compare ourselves to people who are doing better than us, not those who are suffering more.

If we own a 2,500-square-foot house and feel depressed because we don't have a 4,000-square-foot house, this is not real depression. Comparisons with higher social status people allow us to create a victim story about how other people oppress us just by their existence. On the other hand, comparison stories can motivate you to improve your personal circumstances. When viewed properly they can help transform our life.

In Western industrial societies, almost all our basic needs are easy to obtain. Most of the work we do in the name of creating better living conditions is really to improve our social ranking. I am convinced that most modern "depression" is related to social status issues and the comparisons we make. Social media, like Facebook and Instagram, accelerate our social status anxiety stories.

Too often people read, watch, or listen to the news, which accentuates the negative. All the negativity affects them mentally to the point where they feel a need to take medical drugs to cope.

When we fill our minds with doom and gloom all the time, several problems occur in our operating system:

- We become fearful and anxious to the point of not being able to take action.
- We close down and protect ourselves from perceived threats instead of proactively creating a better life.

Swedish teenage activist Greta Thunberg is a good example of someone who has generated stories like this. She talks openly about her fears and anxieties, and it is obvious that her doomsday beliefs are causing her to suffer.

Apocalyptic views of the world are quite destructive, and people buy into them so readily because potential threats appeal to our primal brain. The doomsayers take advantage of our weakness. The people pushing these views are seeking to feel important and control the world to their liking. Just like religious evangelists, they do not have access to all of reality. To presume that their apocalyptical view is the only way to salvation is just as bad. Adults who use children to push agendas that placate their insecurities are among the most evil among us.

The results of doomsday prophecies time after time are proven false. Yet, doomsayers are never held accountable. They plead that their predictions of destruction are just off a little.

If you believe in the end times, the following information might not be helpful. Many people don't know the facts because doomsayers have had the upper hand in brainwashing the young. News media and groups with apocalyptical views dominate our airways. Many people have not been exposed to good news.

I worked as a scientist for nearly four decades and have seen many inventions that will make life better once commercialized. I have read many scientific journals that prove the genius of our species to solve problems.

There has never been a better time to live on the planet. People live longer, healthier lives than ever in human history. A hundred years ago famine and starvation and childhood disease were prevalent. In the early 1800s, 46 percent of the newborns died before the age of five. Today, a fraction of 1 percent does.[13] Obesity is the world's fastest-growing problem because of the abundance of food. Evolution has not caught up with technological changes that make famine no longer a prime worry.

There aren't as many wars as there used to be and so there are fewer casualties. It was only seventy-five years ago that over 70 million people died in war. Death from violent domestic crime is also decreasing rapidly.[14]

Life has gotten better. When people compare themselves to others who are better off financially, they should take advantage

---

13   https://www.statista.com/statistics/1041693/
united-states-all-time-child-mortality-rate/

14   https://www.cdc.gov/nchs/hus/contents2018.htm?search=Homicide,

of the technology literally at their fingertips. The tiny smartphone we carry everywhere connects us with all the worlds' knowledge and wisdom. Even the world's poorest people have access to these devices. We can transform our lives through the internet. The knowledge and opportunities available abound. I know this because I've paid people to work for me in many other countries.

Wealth creation is not a zero-sum game. *"Since 1750 the gross world output has increased more than seventeen hundred times, while the world population has increased only six times."*[15]

In the developed world people have more leisure time and the freedom to use that time in any manner we desire. They can travel pretty much at will around much of the world.

In 2019 the *Spectator* published the article "We've Just Had The Best Decade in Human History" *by* Matt Ridley (author of *The Rational Optimist*). The article debunks the doomsday predictions of the environmental movement.

Humans have never had it so good, and the future looks even brighter.

If things seem hopeless to you, maybe you have a story based on the wrong information and are too engaged in making comparisons. Possibly you are being influenced by your amygdala-generated fears confirming the end is neigh.

When I was in high school in the sixties a literature teacher introduced me to the Zero Population Growth cult and Paul Ehrlich. His apocalyptical book *The Population Bomb* was spreading fear through zero-sum thinking. He predicted that a billion people were going to starve to death due to famine by 1975.

Like today's young people who are worried about "climate change," I was gripped with fear and wrote several papers about this in high school. As I grew older I discovered that people like Ehrlich are everywhere and are still predicting doom, death, and disaster.

---

15   · Paul Zane Pilser, *Unlimited Wealth* (Simon & Schuster, 1990).

It turns out the opposite is true. Higher population produces better solutions to the world's problems. The doom Ehrlich predicted existed only in his mind. Since that time, scientists have produced better seed technology that has reduced pesticide use, improved yields, and has produced foods with better nutrition and greater yields—such that today we can feed 2 billion more people than we did in the 1970s. Worries about running out of oil have led scientists to develop technologies like fracking, which make energy abundant, low cost and cleaner.

In real dollars, the price of gasoline is cheaper than it was during the 1960s before the shortages occurred. This should be giving the people who screamed about running out of oil for decades great relief. Instead, they complain that it's going to destroy the environment. Nothing will satisfy those who are always looking for problems.

Throughout all modern history, when we humans see a problem related to our survival as a species, we have a high 100 percent success rate in solving it. I believe that the bottleneck in solving problems is not scientific breakthroughs. It's persuading people to adopt the new technologies.

During college, I worked for two years in a research lab for the mining company Kennecott Copper. I spent one year working on transforming coal into oil. In the second year, I did computer modeling of ocean beds evaluating the cost of extracting copper and gold from nodules on the ocean floor. That was in the 1970s when doomsayers were forecasting the end of oil and shortages of copper. Both of my projects belied their prognosis.

The point is that humans are creators and are so resourceful that we can create solutions to any problem we need to. Just tell a new story that gets the results you want and don't sit around fretting about the end of the world or screaming, "How Dare You!" at those who are really solving problems.

21

STRESS TESTING: HORMESIS FOR THE MIND

WHEN WRITING COMPUTER code, the computer does not care what the code is. It is there to execute the tasks put forth by the coder and is neutral to the results it gets.

Before software goes "live" it needs to be stress tested to check how it operates in a real-life environment. Similarly, when we live our life we are tested continuously through suffering, disease, and death.

If you've gotten this far, you realize by now that feeling sad is the result of a story. Life is full of suffering, and there are many events that cause us to create stories that allow us to feel sad. After talking about how our stories affect us one of my children asked if it was okay to feel sad. The next morning a forty-year-old radio sports commentator told a story of losing four children when his wife went into premature labor. I felt deeply saddened by his story and actually wept when I heard him tell it.

Just three weeks prior I had experienced joy listening to this man describe his elation when he found out his wife was pregnant with quadruplets after years of infertility issues. Having gone through this same process, I empathized with both his joy and sadness.

In my forties, I went through several years where I believed I was depressed. I went to counseling and took the required anti-depressant drugs to "cure" me. Nothing seemed to get me out of my funk. In one group therapy session, which devolved into a complaint session about how unfair life was, I realized I wasn't really depressed. I was resentful, angry, and felt trapped. Feeling trapped is a theme that has popped up often in my life. It took the conversation in Sam's NYC condo to put the final nail in the coffin on my trapped stories.

It seems that a lot of depression is just anger turned on ourselves. We give ourselves permission to experience any emotion we want. It is important whenever we experience an emotion like sadness to go back and reexamine that story and the results it is producing over the long term.

Sometimes people go through losses like losing a child that causes them to grieve for very long times. If sadness or grief turns into depression, then it is time to reevaluate what story you want to tell.

Suffering is just not something we should accept and look at with exasperation. There is also a redemptive aspect to it. It is a necessary part of accomplishing noble goals, as you will see in Chapter 48.

Many of you may have heard what doesn't kill you makes you stronger. This old adage is based on the biological process called hormesis. Hormesis is the process of cells responding to stress. If the stress is at a level we can physically and mentally handle, we get stronger in response to that stress. If the stress is too great, we get overwhelmed and die. The following graph illustrates the concept. I will discuss the health aspect in Chapter 30.

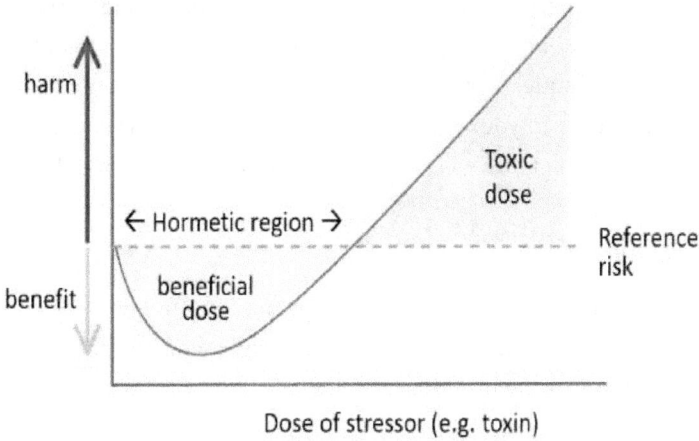

Dose of stressor (e.g. toxin)

Through hormesis evolution has provided us with a way out of suffering. The code we need to write into our story is to find purpose. As we discussed in Chapter 7, having purpose creates joy and happiness in our lives. When people are in mourning, they lose focus on goals and enter a wandering stage.

Many times a family member will find a greater purpose in the death of a child. One example is that of Andrew Pollack whose daughter, Meadow, was killed in the Parkland school massacre. He wrote a book and became an advocate for increasing the safety in our schools.

It may seem cruel to say the universe or reality doesn't care about our pain, but accepting this truth allows us to find new beginnings and put the past behind us. This doesn't mean forgetting the past. It means deciding what part of those events to remember and choosing new meaning for the parts you do remember

Indian-American entrepreneur Naval Ravikant *said, "Reality is neutral. Reality has no judgments. To a tree, there is no concept of right or wrong, good or bad. You're born, you have a whole set of sensory experiences . . . and then you die. How you choose to interpret that is up to you. And you do have a choice."*

Naval's statement is an empowering viewpoint on how we can live our lives and not get stuck in emotional stories of suffering.

We all suffer a great deal in life. Don't become a drama queen with regards to your ordeals and think you alone have the worst life. In Chapter 38 I will cover how to be grateful for your adversity.

Next Steps

Want to hear more about flaws in our thinking and how to extract ourselves from them? Go to rebootmystories.com for more information on wrong thinking.

PART V

Unlocking the Code
to Transformation

"I'm working on my life story. I'm not decided if it's going to be a musical or a movie with music in it."

—Dolly Parton

22

A REPROGRAMMING EXAMPLE

THE STORY OF my life as a parent could have taken a much different turn. I come from a family of eight children, and my first wife was one of seven children. So we fully expected to have a large family when we married.

Throughout our thirties, we attempted to have children the old-fashioned way without success. We had to endure endless personal examinations and several painful surgeries over about a five-year period. We had to endure the constant questioning about when we were going to have children while pretending the questions didn't' hurt us.

After years of infertility treatments, we finally gave up. For many people, this is a devastating story. After all, reproducing is the primary evolutionary directive. To fail at this purpose is the largest possible failure a human can have. It seemed especially cruel having both been from such large families. Even sex had turned into a chore as the anticipation and joy of becoming a parent disappeared.

There is lots of blame to go around when big problems like this happen. It's easy to blame your spouse, your parents, even God. Infertility ends many marriages or leads to addictive behavior to numb the pain.

Briefly, I thought about finding another wife. Culturally it seemed like a logical course of action. Even the Catholic Church, which opposes divorce, decrees infertility as a valid reason for annulling a marriage. But we had been exposed to a lot of motivational and positive thinking books. With such possibility thinking, we were able to reframe what it meant to be a parent from just the biological definition. We told ourselves a new story that the joy in parenting doesn't come from genes. We could find happiness in raising a child not biologically related to us.

But as we explored our options "experts" told us it would be at least a five-year wait to adopt an infant. I was forty at the time. The idea of being a new dad at forty-five sickened me. It was almost enough to turn us into pessimists, but we didn't buy the experts storylines. We decided to explore new avenues. We advertised in small-town newspapers across the country for pregnant women looking to give up their child for adoption. We networked in adoption groups, and we found adoption agencies that catered to specific clientele that had infants that did not meet their clients' needs.

We measured the results by the responses we got in our outreach, not by what the experts or the gossips told us. This was a feedback loop and the 80/20 Principle at work.

Within nine months after making the decision to adopt, we brought home our first son. Within sixteen months we had three infants in diapers running around the house because we created the story we wanted. My training changing my sibling's diapers finally paid off!

We didn't allow ourselves to be victims or indulge in a pity party about our poor genetics. We didn't allow ourselves to get depressed or even blame anyone. We told a new story about how we could get what we desired. We took action and used feedback to get better and better at finding a way to get what we wanted.

I would be lying to say that my life was transformed completely by this experience (except of course the parenting part did change my life). It is only in retrospect that I see clearly what we did and why it worked.

Reviewing the successful events in your life can be just as valuable as reviewing triggers. At that time, I was knee-deep in changing diapers again and took no time to reflect. It is only after finding a system to analyze events that this came into focus for me.

The following are some frameworks we used to achieve this. Changing your mindset is not necessarily easy. When we started going out in public with two infant boys, people would regularly ask if they were twins. When we told them the boys were three months apart they would look perplexed for several minutes, searching for some explanation. The obvious answer eluded them.

When you utilize the Debugging Software you will be baffled sometimes. Hopefully, some of this will help you.

23

RE-FRAMING THE META-STORY OF YOUR LIFE

THE DEBUGGING SOFTWARE works well to address issues that trigger you in life but doesn't really say much about how to approach life and create overarching storylines.

Think of the daily stories you create as small subroutines inside a much larger algorithm controlling your life. For example, the algorithm that runs Facebook uses deep psychology to get you addicted to keep the Facebook app open many hours of the day. A subroutine inside that algorithm may show you advertising of something you recently viewed on Amazon with the intent of selling a particular product.

The illustration below depicts how our stories are built on layers of much larger stories.

Universal Archetype

Tribal Frame

Personal Story

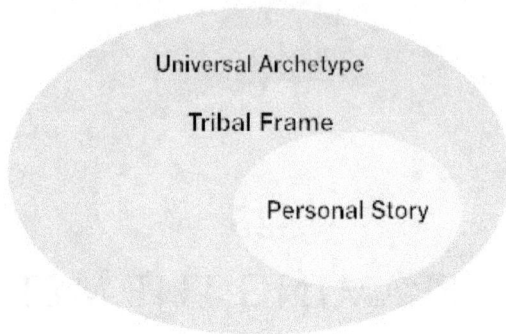

Carl Jung described archetypes as the collective unconsciousness that humans share. Jordan Peterson talks about this extensively in the YouTube video series I cited earlier on the psychological significance of the biblical stories.

It is because of the universally shared stories we have that we can connect with people who are completely different from us. Disney movies are famous for incorporating archetypical myths into the plotline—the reason these films are so enduring. I recommend reading Joseph Campbell's book the *Power of Myth*.

Below the universal archetypes is what I call tribal frameworks that start to create subplots in the human story.

The word *frame* when used as a verb means:

> *To contrive, devise or compose as a poem*
> *To fashion or shape*
> *To shape or adapt for a particular purpose*

Tribal frames weave another layer of complexity into our stories. A tribal group is an association of people with common links, attributes, or interests. We create tribal affiliations with race, culture, gender, age, nationality, religion, political affiliation, the type of work you do, and much more. Your family is your strongest tribal frame.

For example, I am a man (tribe 1), grew up in a large family (tribe 2), and attended Catholic churches and schools (tribe 3). The family was lower middle class (tribe 4) and aligned with the Democrat party (tribe 5). I worked for a large corporation (tribe 6). I am an American (tribe 7) and of European-Caucasian descent (tribe 8). That is just for starters.

Throughout my life, I entered and then left various tribes: college tribes, married people tribes, parents of adopted children tribe, step-parent tribe, an Amway multi-level marketing tribe, and bicycling tribes. I am currently in a tribe of people traveling full time in an RV. Even in this tribe, people who travel in expensive Class A RVs see themselves in a different tribe from people in camper trailers or those in fifth-wheel trailers.

Each of these tribal affiliations influences my stories on a daily basis. For example, at one time in my life, I denounced religion and became an atheist. Even so, my stories continued to largely reflect the mores of Catholicism and Western Civilization (largely developed on the back of religious beliefs).

Most people live their lives totally boxed in by the frames set by the tribal groups they grew up in and never examine other possibilities. We are often imprinted with stories from these tribal connections very early. Sometimes the tribal affiliation is so great it's difficult to see, much less escape.

Most people never even question these meta-frames or worldviews, because they are 100 percent certain that their tribal frames are "right." Megan Phelps-Roger was a member of the Westboro Baptist Church. Her family would famously go to funerals and protest gays in a very ugly manner. Yet, in her memoir *Unfollow*, Phelps-Roger described her family as 100 percent certain of their righteousness.

You may vote for a certain political party just because your parents did, for example. You may have sexual anxieties because of some religious teaching from your youth. Believing you are stuck with a certain frame is the pattern your mind created to conserve energy.

The Debugging Software helps to identify what triggers you and is mostly focused on personal stories. Like fish in water, people do not question the frame that their tribal groups encoded them with. When examined on their own, people often completely miss the frame that may have caused the trigger. But when confronted with the problem of their frame by others, they may react like a trapped lion.

There are many tribal issues like race, gender, religion, or culture, which dominate our stories. No doubt that each of us has built stories with confirmation biases supporting one or more of those tribal frames.

Some of our tribal stories that shape the concepts I discuss will appear inside these frames. Any one of these is likely to invoke a strong negative reaction in you. Pay attention to your reaction when you read through them.

In the Debugging Software, I introduced the concept of the Me story where subconscious issues that caused the initial trigger may come to light. These frames are like Us stories that may be in the unconscious realm of our psyche.

Changes here can make the largest impact to the life story that we create. When you go through your Debugging Software, ponder whether any of these may be holding you back from creating the story you desire. I'm not sure it is possible to go beyond the universal archetype, but I am certain that you can go beyond your tribal frames.

To begin this process, I suggest listing all of the tribes, current and past, that may be influencing your stories. Here are some examples from my life:

Tribe	Potential Influences on My Stories
Gender	Stories about relationships with woman Stories about sex and porn Stories about how a man should act Stories about my body and my appearance Stories about chivalry
Race	Stories about how other races interact with my race Stories about how I view other races
Family	Stories about how family relationships work My first stories about money Stories of parent-child relationship Stories about how to raise children Stories about food and diet
Religion	Stories about sex and marriage Stories about God and religions Stories about right and wrong Stories about how I should treat others
Amway	Stories about entrepreneurship More stories about money Stories about self-reliance Stories about leadership Stories about positive mental attitude Stories about persistence Stories about learning
Cycling	Stories about health Stories about what is possible
Political Party	Stories about how government should work Stories about which groups should be helped by government

Work	Stories about teamwork
	Stories about leadership
	Stories about providing value
	Stories about commitment

These are just a few examples from my tribal influences. In the following sections, I explore a more in-depth analysis of some of these stories.

One of the dangers of being too strongly linked to our tribal stories is that we create an "us versus "them" frame when dealing with others. It's easy to fall into a tribal trap. I've mentioned that evil politicians use identity politics to divide us. Work on growing beyond your tribal identities if you want to become a better human.

24

STAYING POSITIVE
AND FOCUSED

WHEN WE CONTEMPLATE the pain and suffering that goes on in the world, it is hard not to have a negative outlook. In fact, our evolutionary biology may have imprinted negative thinking into our survival mechanism. The media, doomsday groups and religious groups reinforce this negative outlook. The book of Revelation in the Bible speaks of a coming day of judgment. Groups like the Club of Rome and Malthusians continuously predict bad times ahead. Like Christian ministers, they promise punishment for enemies who don't agree with their point of view. The Climate Change doomsday cult is just another iteration of the same obsession. (I call them a cult because only a religious cult would classify those who disagree with their Creed as deniers. Real scientists do not talk like this.)

For the doomsayers, there is always a global crisis that is going to kill us.

Yet, what does it gain us if all our stories are negative?

Looking at the results of this thinking, we can observe a society that is anxious and on edge about events that have no impact on their life. We see people who are afraid to go out in the world and enjoying life or taking a chance at a new experience because they worry that something bad might happen. The result is a society hooked on anti-anxiety medication.

There is a certain truth to the narrative that if we expect bad things to happen, they will. This type of tribal frame will compel us to create stories around prepping for "The End of the World as We Know It" and become "Preppers". It can keep us from the joy of having children because of fear that the world will end in twelve years as US Congresswoman Alexandria Ocasio-Cortez stated.

It also keeps us stuck in a victim story.

Adopting a frame that says, "Yes, I have problems, but they are solvable either on my own or with help" allows us to create stories that are uplifting. It's not what happens to us that matters, it's how we react to it. Look for a reason to give up, and it's there. Look for a solution, and you will often find it.

Even though someone may have a pessimistic outlook, we are attracted to people who are optimistic and positive and don't like being around people who are negative. Positive people give us hope that we can survive the next apocalypse.

Paradoxically, a Christian minister is most famous for promoting this point of view. Norman Vincent Peale's book *The Power of Positive Thinking* is the seminal text on this perspective. Joel Osteen is Peale's modern-day equivalent. He attracts millions every Sunday to his optimistic sermons.

Two hundred years ago it made sense to have a negative outlook. You had to be prepared for crop failure or wars or early death from disease. In modern times, there is much more upside to having a positive outlook and little downside risk. There is little risk of a tiger attack or a rival tribe seeking to plunder your town. We go about our lives in relative safety. A positive outlook opens our minds to new solutions to problems. We are more likely to see opportunities to make money. Positive people are happier and live longer than negative people. When you have a positive outlook the possibility increases that you will do and achieve far more in life and be more richly rewarded for it.

My wife and I enjoy biking. In my early sixties, I decided I wanted to bike in Colorado. I had never biked in the mountains, so we joined a bike tour, which offered a supported route over eight mountain peaks in seven days.

Although we had tried to train for a couple of months prior to our trip, the first few days were agony due to the elevation. My wife suffered altitude sickness on the fourth day of the tour after summiting a 12,126-foot peak and had to drop out.

The final day of the tour was a climb up Pikes Peak at 14,110 feet of elevation. This was about two thousand feet higher than any other mountain we had climbed during the week.

The bicyclists in the tour were mostly extremely fit and in their thirties and forties with only a handful of riders older than me.

Surprisingly, less than half of the two hundred participants chose to ride up Pikes Peak and half of those that started made it to the summit. I saw many riders on their ten-thousand-dollar carbon bikes turn around at twelve thousand feet when the grade started to get very steep.

The week before the tour started my wife and I had driven to the summit. I could barely walk I was so dizzy from the altitude. The task of biking up the mountain with its hairpin curves and steep cliffs along the roadway (without guardrails) seemed impossible. When I reached thirteen thousand feet that Saturday my bike was wobbling all over the road. The tour operator insisted that I stop.

I stood there for twenty minutes gasping for breath. I knew the summit was only a mile away and was determined to ride there. Like many other decisions in my life, I was entirely focused on the end result and the emotions or suffering in between were irrelevant.

So I shook the tour operator off and kept at it. I was the next to last person who summited that day. I only surpassed a seventy-six-year-old rider. The power of thinking positively exceeded what I had physically trained to do.

I'm sure that many of the riders that turned around or did not even start had the physical ability to make the summit. But they did not have the positive mental story.

When you are positive and focused on a task, the obstacles fade away. The pain diminishes. When the task is especially challenging, the dopamine rush you get blanks out all the trials and tribulations.

When a negative person achieves the calamity they predicted, there is no dopamine hit. The result is disappointing. Being able to say, "See, I told ya" is not fulfilling. It gives us no joy.

As Maslow's hierarchy shows us, humans love to be around aspirational people. Stay positive and focused.

25

SEEING ABUNDANCE

GROWING UP, MY dad set the tone for how I learned to think about money. I heard phrases like, "Money doesn't grow on trees." "Shut the lights off, do you think I am a bank?" And "Clean your plate. Children in China are starving."

I remember an event at one of many family trips with ten of us crammed in a station wagon and hours of driving to visit relatives. We had stopped for a meal. The waitress tried to take orders from a table with eight restless and noisy children, including a screaming infant. One of my siblings had the temerity to order a large orange juice. My dad lost it in the restaurant in a very embarrassing way, letting us know that it cost too much to get a large juice! The lesson I learned: we couldn't have what we wanted.

So I quickly viewed my life as one of scarcity and lack.

In the eighties, my father introduced me to a company called Amway. It was the first time I learned about entrepreneurship. I never heard the term at home or at school. Amway Corporation sold household products using a multi-level sales model. People who became distributors acted as independent contract employees, owning their own businesses. These individual businesses aggregated into tribes, which held seminars and rallies to train and motivate people associated with their tribe.

During that time I had the opportunity to hear economist and bestselling author of *Unlimited Wealth* Paul Zane Pilzer speak. His talk revolutionized how I thought about money and wealth. After listening to his talk and absorbing his book, it demolished the stories my father had programmed into me in my youth. Pilzer's views governed in the story of creating my own family where I saw that there was unlimited potential to adopt infants—not the story of lack of supply the world preached. I found so many unwanted children that I was able to adopt another four siblings a few years after the first three.

Classical economics is based on the belief that resources are limited and that humans are destined to fight over how to distribute a limited pie. Life described this way is a zero-sum game resulting in envy and endless bloodshed.

If you look at the world before 1750, that was principally true. Most of the people lived pretty much the same as they had for millennia. Like the other exponential curves I discussed earlier, the human knowledge growth curve plodded along with little or no improvement for millennia but then exploded in the nineteenth century.

Today we live exceedingly rich lives compared to those in 1750. There are 6 billion more people consuming the planet's riches, yet the amount of resources in the world has not decreased. In fact, we have more resources now than ever!

Pilzer's formula describes wealth as a product of resources and technology. Because this is a product formula ($W = R \times T$), the more technology advances, the greater the effect on wealth becomes. As an example, humans turned something once thought to be worthless (sand) into trillions of dollars of wealth (silicon wafers and computers).

Pilzer also recognized that humans could redefine what a resource actually is, and we are not limited to physical resources in the ground. For example, the Internet is a resource that we can apply technology to in order to create more wealth. This resource, which only appeared recently in modern history, is an example of Pilzer's foresight.

So we create resources, which can create more resources to solve problems. This power law effect means that solutions far outpace problems. Today we are often in search of problems to solve. This is an astounding way to think about abundance instead of scarcity!

Doomsayers assured us for years that we were running out of oil and food. Yet, advances like genetically modified organisms—seeds that have been modified to resist pests and droughts or provide Vitamin A—and fracking have turned food and energy into abundant resources. These are just two examples of thousands I've observed that bust the old economic model of a fixed pie.

The Internet has been one of the greatest technological advances created that can equalize opportunities to create wealth. With a smartphone, anyone in the world can access a market of billions of people and create solutions that solve problems.

New technology creates new problems and people will always be willing to pay someone to solve their problems. In fact, the whole of free-market capitalism is all about solving problems for other people. The bigger the problem, the more people are willing to pay to solve it. Those who solve the most problems get the richest. Looking at yourself as a problem solver instead of an employee will reframe how you perform and grow.

This is why STEM majors in college tend to make more than English literature students. Technology companies are willing to pay more to a STEM major because they solve big problems. As a chemical engineer, I never worried about not having an income (I had promises of a job any time I wanted to leave DuPont). Too many companies had problems and not enough problem solvers.

We can choose to see the world from the frame of abundance and admire those who have solved the largest problems (and gotten rewarded for that effort). When we adopt this frame, we will start to see opportunities everywhere. And we will see those people who take advantage of these opportunities in a different light.

People who see the world in a scarcity mindset create stories of envy and lack. They obsess about redistributing others' wealth and spend their time on activism in groups like Occupy Wall Street and Extinction Rebellion.

There is a mistaken belief that governments can create wealth and distribute it to the populace. Wealth only comes from creating new products or services and it is only a free people that create. Governments distort the process or suppress it by regulations, but do not create wealth. Oppressed people try to copy and steal others' inventions. Entrepreneurs will create the next Apple computer or Tesla and will be the ones to solve climate and environmental issues.

I've seen this all over the world. When I traveled to Russia in 1997 to adopt, I had to bring staples and staplers for the local governments to use. The adoption papers we were given were typed on a manual typewriter and sown together. We were trapped in an apartment for four days with no running water because the city pump broke and there were no spares. The luxury train we traveled on was powered by coal and soot filled our cabin. Our elite leaders treat Russia as a great superpower, but Russia's treatment of entrepreneurs and wealth creation reveals them as a bankrupt third-world country.

Finally, note that the Bible does not say, "Money is the root of all evil." It says, "The *love* of money is the root of all evil." You can see money as a measure of how much value you deliver your fellow human beings and a resource to create even more for the world and help others.

26

STAYING IN LOVE WITH LIFE

HUMANS ARE IN awe of creation. There is very much a collective archetype surrounding the belief that there is a divine architect. This reverence for the unexplainable has metamorphosed into cult-like groups that have been both simultaneously uplifting and disastrous for millions of people throughout history.

For many, the devotion to God or Buddha or Allah or other deities has created a sense of purpose. Undoubtedly the most beautiful artwork, music, and architecture have been created out of love for this being.

On the other hand, many have died in wars fought in the name of some religious deity. And countless have been persecuted by evil people pretending to be the mediator to the almighty.

People who grow up in controlling cult-like religious groups often rebel against the dogma when they get older. Many become militant atheists who transfer their belief from a religion to a material or social cause. One example is the belief in multi-verses (a belief that our universe is one of infinite universes) to explain reality. There is no more evidence for multi-verses than there is for a god. Even atheists cannot escape the need to believe in something.

I grew up in a large, Catholic family and attended Catholic grade school and then a Catholic high school. So I was pretty well indoctrinated with Catholic ideology well into my teens. At one time, I even thought I wanted to be a priest. When I left home and attended college I was like many who grow up with strict religious upbringing. I rebelled and proclaimed myself an atheist. Looking back at this now, I am sure this rebellion was primarily against the church's strict restrictions around sex and marriage.

I maintained my atheistic viewpoint until my thirties when I started an Amway business. The first events I attended shocked me. People on stage talked about God. I would leave the conference room whenever a speaker got overly religious in my opinion.

One of the tenets pushed by the Amway business leaders was that leaders are readers. So I took up the habit of reading three to four positive thinking and self-help books a month over the next ten years. I eventually came upon the book *The Road Less Travelled* by M.Scott Peck. It appealed to me, and I eventually read all of Peck's books in the order that he wrote them. He wrote of his transition from atheist to someone interested in Eastern religions (Buddhism, Taoism) and then to Christianity. His arguments made total sense to me and actually mirrored my transitions in beliefs. He helped me accept a religious belief as an important component to being a human.

That a particular organization has all the answers and can save us, however, is at odds with my worldview that we should not play the victim. Myriad rules give power to the leaders and disempower the congregation. But belonging to religious groups is not synonymous with having awe regarding the universe and how it came to be.

The Ten Commandments provide guidance to people to keep them from doing evil. The commandments did not say do this or else. Humans added the "or else" as a way to control others. Religious leaders proclaim their own "or else" with threats of eternal damnation to a place no one can verify exists. I think there are a great number of leaders of religious groups whose fear of the unknown prompts them to control the chaos they see. People who are drawn to religions often are looking for some kind of security to make sense of the world. Groups craft rules prohibiting activities like drinking or dancing in response to their internal fears.

If you examine the root of the major religions before humans distort it, there is the idea of love.

The way forward is not to reject the idea of a God or Creator and the inborn impulse to worship or be in awe of something greater than us. I find listening to spiritual music during a religious service extremely uplifting. There is something universal inside us that urges us to enter into this spiritual realm. We want to be loved and if belief in the supernatural can satisfy the desire, there is good in it.

There is a tremendous collection of stories about human encounters with the spiritual world. Many have come through visions seen during prayer or meditation, some from hallucinogens, and others from near-death experiences. But they all have very common themes of being one with all and love for all and all three groups experience profound changes as a result.

Those who have experienced the spiritual realm create new stories of peace and acceptance of the world and their fellow humans. The most common effect of these encounters is a feeling of love, which the great spiritual leaders also teach. Most people who go through these experiences are transformed and are no longer triggered by little things.

I believe it is very helpful to include in your story the possibility of a universal spiritual life force at work that is based on love. But be careful not to be seduced by cult-like groups that use a tyrannical approach to spirituality.

The bottom line is that having a spiritual component in one's life produces better results on the whole than having only a physical story. And the objective of holding stories in our mind is to produce results that benefit us long term. Part of the benefit of a spiritual story is the idea of staying connected, which I touch on a little later in Chapter 37. It appears we are connected via quantum phenomena. Religions have postulated that point of view for millennia.

Like many scientists, I spent years rejecting religion. However, the deeper I explored science, the more I came to be in awe of the universe and more in alignment with a spiritual outlook. Whether viewing images of the galaxy, cellular biology, or quantum physics, I am always awed by the complexity and richness of all that can be seen.

And if we are part of a simulation, as some propose, then there has to be a prime programmer. But why would we want to worship Larry P. in the software development department?

In addition to opening us to the possibility of connection with each other and exposure to the awesomeness of creation, one of Christianity's great contributions to humanity is the concept of redemption. Redemption is the ultimate act of love. It is the act of offsetting a defect. To forgive and accept the possibility that someone who has hurt others can change is a noble quality. The rejection of this possibility with the "cancel culture" is a step backward in living a happy story.

When we forgive someone, we don't hold a grudge against them. They're just a symbol of our inner turmoil that we project our feelings onto. Our anger cannot change the past. Forgiveness is primarily a story about ourselves.

I had to go through a process of forgiveness for the lady next door who tormented me by calling me homely. Once I understood the concept of projection, I came to realize that she must have had her own demons, which drove her to bully a young child. I moved away from home as a teen and never interacted with her again. Yet for years I carried around anger about how she had hurt me. Did my anger impact her at all? No. It was only eating at me. Forgiveness is much more for our own mental and physical health than it is for the other person.

The process of confession is admitting that we have participated in creating the suffering in the world. As Dostoyevsky indicates in his books, we are all implicated in the evil around us. We need to acknowledge our role to bring about our redemption. In Chapter 47 I talk about the hero's journey. Heroes always experience a dark night of the soul, and their turning point comes about with redemption.

I suggest we create stories where we see our fellow humans as flawed and doing the best they can with their level of consciousness. And if they screw up (in our lofty self-righteous opinion) then we should be so gracious as to forgive them rather than "cancel" them.

When we can be gracious with other people and see them as flawed individuals like us, it is possible to love them and not criticize or condemn them. For what we see in them is a reflection of our inner self.

27

STAYING IN THE PRESENT

---

*"Therefore the Master acts without doing anything
and teaches without saying anything.
Things arise and she lets them come; things
disappear, and she lets them go.
She has but doesn't possess, acts but doesn't expect.
When her work is done she forgets it.
That is why it lasts forever."*

—Lao Tzu - *Tao Te Ching*

WHEN WE WORK through the Debugging Software, we may notice that many of our triggers are related to guilt about past events or anxiety about what may happen in the future.

What is strange about this is that time only exists in the present moment. Because there is only now, it seems like it would be natural to just exist in the present. Yet, for some reason, it is a very difficult state to stay in.

Our brains develop endless thoughts. Where these thoughts originate is not known. However, we do know that our amygdala reacts to these thoughts by constantly evaluating potential threats the stream of thoughts present to our minds. Our runaway thoughts are often what triggers us into creating a story without an event. For example, during the COVID-19 pandemic, many young people were triggered by fear and hid in their homes tweeting memes of the outdoor air filled with viruses. In reality, the disease almost exclusively targeted the elderly or very unhealthy populations and the outdoors was the healthiest place to be.[16]

The opposite of reacting is observing. Meditation is the practice of learning to observe thoughts and let them go. For decades monks seclude themselves away from worldly distractions, learning how to meditate; it's not an easy practice.

Meditation carried out successfully is a way to bypass the programming of OS-Me. It is outside the program like a coder is outside of the code. A coder can create a piece of software, press the "start" button and observe what results the program produces. When we are in a place where we can simply observe thoughts, we will not get triggered. We can be as dispassionate as the coder. The sixth century BC Chinese philosophical text *Tao Te Ching*, by Lao Tzu, explains this concept the best.

When we are triggered, we assess the trigger as good or bad. As Lao Tzu writes:

"When people see some things as beautiful, other things become ugly.
When people see some things as good, other things become bad."

Being free of judgment—not seeing events as good or bad—is the key to success in meditation. The power in meditation comes from awareness and understanding of where the mind is going.

I wrote about the duality of our system hardware in Chapter 8. One side focused on self-interest, the other on connection. Our negativity bias challenges our brains to find good and to thrive.

---

16   . Sunshine kills viruses and large fluid volumes dilute the concentrations of any virus particles. Air has the largest volume of fluid on the planet.

We are able to enjoy happiness only because of the intense sadness we have experienced. We constantly make decisions about risk versus safety.

The mind clings to our views and fights this duality, but the observer in us notices it. The mind wants to create a story that one side is better than the other. Our mind can conserve energy if there is one pattern that can be applied for future events. Our triggers are a battle of judgment about the way things should be based on a pattern our mind has adopted as truth. When we cling to that old model, we forge conflict in ourselves. Observing releases us from the conflict.

For example, we may cling to a political (or is it religious?) belief that our party is the righteous one and those who belong to the other party are dancing with the devil. This creates tremendous political conflict to the point where family members disown each other over who they voted for. The observer can see the good and bad in each party and not get triggered by opposing political views.

A secondary benefit of meditation is expanding the time gap between the trigger and our response. The Debugging Software is an attempt to train our mind to respond with our frontal cortex instead of our amygdala. The more we meditate and train our mind to observe our thoughts and extend the time between observation and reaction, the more capable we will be of responding with our cortex.

Meditation slows our train of thought to a point where the frontal cortex can jump in front of the amygdala and avoid the train wreck the reptile brain was preparing for. It also will help us hear our inner voice more easily. The reason we often fail to hear our inner guide is due to the clutter from too much random noise in our code. My dad always suggested counting to ten before reacting. That is the simplest form of meditation that can allow us to hear the voice of reason.

Even if we do not become a Zen master, routine meditation

will still benefit us. Studies have noted meditation will reduce stress, anxiety, blood pressure, and provide clearer thinking. I am not an expert, but I've practiced meditation daily during periods of my life that were chaotic and found it to be quite helpful in calming me and providing clarity of thought. After meditation, I've found that within a few seconds of a triggering event I can let the thoughts pass and not have the emotional reaction I once had.

I have especially found it useful in getting to sleep quickly. I am able to let go of the day's problems in a few minutes and free my mind for a restful night of sleep.

✦

Meditation is like hypnosis, in that it guides the thought patterns in your mind to stay in the present. Imagine if your car radio played all the stations simultaneously. You couldn't understand anything. Meditation separates the stations and lets us understand them. In meditation, we become detached from the radio stations.

When hypnotized, your mind focuses on one thing, like tuning to one radio station. You become hyper-focused. Hypnosis suppresses the voices of doubt and fear that are playing on the other stations.

People who are open to suggestion are good subjects for hypnosis. They are the ones cured by sugar pills in double-blind drug trials. In active self-hypnosis, people can direct themselves to focus on an outcome they desire.

Michael Jordan tells how in his mid-thirties, after already winning several championships, he used a self-hypnosis technique to help him improve. Before a game he would sit in the locker room repeating to himself, "They say you are too old. They say you are too old. They say you are too old." He would repeat that mantra until he was angry and determined to prove them wrong.

That exercise caused him to play with such ferocity to prove his greatness that he would crush the younger players.

Many of the techniques self-help books describe are actually a form of self-hypnosis. Visualizations, affirmations, acting as if you're already confident or successful work if you have a receptive mind. Some people are very open to this and convince themselves of the truth of the mantra, like Jordan, and go on to great success. For those who are skeptical, this type of motivation doesn't work. Skepticism is a trigger for you indicating an unresolved issue around trust. Work on that and likely self-hypnosis will work for you.

Freedom comes from understanding where problems come from, not the conscious attempt to end them. Our minds are at once the cause of our problems and the solution.

28

ACCEPTING OTHERS

THE BIBLE TELLS you to "Judge not that you be not judged" (Matt. 7:1), yet we judge each other all the time. It's actually a skill that allows us to survive as a species. In past human history to judge a threat incorrectly frequently led to death.

Judging is a deeply ingrained pattern in our thinking. A reflexive reaction by many who think themselves "woke" is to not judge anyone or anything. To be non-judgmental, though, is a flawed response. It is to repress a survival skill. We must be able to discern foe from friend and good from bad.

When I write of judging, I am speaking about observing what results an event produces and determining if those results fit your purpose. There is a duality around this judging. We assign the labels good or bad to everything we see. In contrast, observing does not assign a value. So anytime we judge, we make an assessment as to whether or not something is unacceptable to us.

The first aspect of judging is to determine the threat level. This has prime importance when discerning whether a tiger plans to attack or someone in another tribe is hoping to take your land.

Another aspect of judging is to determine if the behaviors you observe are beneficial or detrimental to your own well-being. Washing your hands is a behavior that benefits us in fighting disease. The results of excess alcohol consumption are detrimental to our health. We can judge that overeating and lack of exercise can also hurt our health.

However, the judging we most commonly engage in has nothing to do with these two aspects. The dark side of judging involves our desire for status.

Social status is important because it determines who gets the prized breeding partner. Over time it has evolved to determine someone's worthiness compared to others. I've written about how we have a tendency to hurt others to make ourselves feel superior. We do that in our own minds in regards to our social status.

To impose our social status rules on others we craft all kinds of rules and modes of conduct. Zoning laws that ban low-income housing or require so many acres per plot is an example of judging based on status. Clothing is another status symbol. We buy certain brands of clothes or accessories to show we are more successful and superior to others.

Judging others about the dress they are wearing or the color of their skin or their politics is non-productive in terms of personal growth. People with high levels of education and wealth are often motivated by social status. Their perceived status is a way to justify their sanctimonious behavior. The rich and highly educated are not better than others. Their hearts are as dark as the rest of us, and they are just as responsible for the evil in the world.

Imagine living in a large estate surrounded by high walls and protected by security guards. You have every conceivable luxury and are chauffeured around in a limousine. The streets around your mansion are filled with homeless people, discarded needles, and human feces. You ignore those people and do nothing to help them. Are those around your estate who are suffering worse human beings? Are you better? Can you envision how both parties might be contributing to the suffering in the world?

Judging others often involves lots of mind reading. We often judge others based solely on what we think they are thinking. We have no idea what other people are thinking because we do not know their stories. When we judge people, we reflexively judge whether they are meeting a standard we set in our mind. In other words, we are projecting our internal thought pattern or world-view onto them. It's subjective to our own thoughts and beliefs.

When we judge results, we objectively determine if the attribute we are judging produces the results we want in our life.

The key to keeping yourself on the correct side of judgment is to differentiate between judging others and judging results.

Here is where the concept of acceptance comes in. Accepting others is an observational process. As Lao Tzu describes, accepting the world as it is, is the only path to inner peace. Judging others to elevate our status contributes to the suffering in the world. Fighting for justice or attempting to save others does not give us peace.

Accepting someone does not mean you should enable his or her behavior. We covered why in Chapter 16. Acceptance means viewing reality and assigning only two possible meanings to it:

- There is a threat to my life or property that I must address.
- I can learn from my observations in order to live a healthier, richer or more peaceful life.

When we stop judging others and accept them for who they are, our relationships change. Here are two examples of how I've judged people and how to shift your thoughts:

Judging Thought and Mind Reading	Acceptance Thought
That overweight person is lazy. They have no self-control, eat too much, and don't exercise.	That overweight person is suffering from health issues I do not want. I should change my eating and exercising habits to avoid that. I accept them for who they are and where they are right now. My desire to help them should not be based on the belief that they are bad or helpless.
That poor person is lazy. They spend all their money on cigarettes and booze and dope. Obviously, they want to mooch off the hard workers and just collect welfare checks.	I see that person is suffering from a lack of money. Not having enough money to live comfortably is not the experience I want to have in life, so I need to learn how to make more money. I'll see if they are open to guidance on how to increase their income, but I accept them for where they are and do not believe I am their savior.

29

FINDING INDEPENDENCE

PEOPLE ARE SOCIAL beings. Most of us enter into a relationship in search of something. Whether that is sex, love, validation, friendship, or the fear of being alone, we don't seek companionship in a vacuum.

Why do relationships fail so often? Most often they fail because the relationship does not meet our expectations. We may romanticize a story about finding a "soul mate" who will be perfect for us only to find the reality is quite different.

The problem seems to be that we often form relationships out of neediness rather than real love. Our neediness often stems from childhood traumas that create the Me stories I discussed earlier. Our neediness creates unrealistic expectations that the other person somehow owes us something and should know what that need is. We engage in mind reading about what the other person's actions mean in regard to our expectations. We blame rather than take responsibility.

There are many types of neediness. Some people are so afraid of being alone that they stay in relationships that are abusive.

Other people enjoy toying with people's emotions in order to feel in control. And sometimes two people may complement each other. A complementary relationship may not be needy in the strictest sense if both parties are competent and not strictly reliant on the other. Relationships that are codependent exhibit neediness when each person plays an incompetency game.

I have had a relationship where there was a mutual neediness. I stayed out of my need for a sexual partner, and the women stayed because she wanted validation that she was attractive.

Another way to frame a relationship is to look at it as an opportunity to grow. Expect that the other person will trigger us and expose our Me stories. Expect that the other person is deeply flawed and has many hidden Me stories that you will trigger in them. This is the opposite of a needy relationship. In this type of relationship mutual growth can occur, and you each can reach high levels of satisfaction.

When we see our partner in this light and can explore their Me stories with them, our empathy will increase greatly. We can help each other to not play the victim game. If we can explore our relationship and learn where our Me stories cause us to be needy, we can learn to be independent. Having that independence allows us to weather the storms of any relationship.

Neediness is at its core a form of seeing oneself as powerless to create one's own happiness. When we move beyond our neediness, we can actually find real love and friendship. This will be the greatest gift you can give yourself.

30

STAYING HEALTHY

"Your mind tells you that you want comfort. Your body thrives on discomfort. Too much comfort leads to obesity and ill health. Go beyond your comfort zone."

—PD Mangan

How DO YOU see your body? Is it just a machine that needs to go to the shop (doctor) when the check engine light (pain) comes on? Or do you see it as a priceless vehicle that you must proactively protect and nourish?

Do you see your body conditions as out of your control run by your genetics? Do you view exercise and a healthy diet as a grind?

Our mind and body are intricately connected. The health of the body affects the mind and poor mental hygiene can detrimentally affect our bodies.

While it is patently obvious that our genetics plays a role in our health, it's also equally obvious that we have a major impact on our health by the habits we choose. Remember, genetics is responsible for only 5 to 10 percent of our health.

What we eat, how we exercise, our personal hygiene, our sleep quality, the type of risks we take, and how we choose to react to stress all are factors in the quality of our health.

We may have a frame that since our parents and siblings have or had certain diseases, we also are a prisoner to that illness. But that is not true. My wife's parents and sibling all suffer from heart disease, stroke, and obesity, yet my wife is perfectly healthy and a little underweight. Not a day goes by when we are not actively biking, hiking, walking, or engaged in some other exercise. We are also very conscious of our nutrition.

No outcome is guaranteed but with 90 to 95 percent control of our health, we can choose to have better health. We can create better stories about our health and body. Living a healthy lifestyle can greatly reduce our suffering. Paying attention to nutrition and exercise helps. Choosing your social circles wisely to avoid toxic people is beneficial. And not neglecting your spirituality will make a difference to your other stories.

Here's a way to look at your health. It's called the "Expensive Tissue Hypothesis."[17] I mentioned earlier that the brain is only 2 percent of our body weight but uses over 20 percent of our energy. Over hundreds of thousands of years of evolution, our brain weight has grown from less than a pound to about three pounds.[18] The trade-off for this larger brain is a smaller gut. Since finding food was hard work, our brain sought to optimize nutrition.

What this larger brain has done is to allow us to find and prepare higher quality food. The term "high quality food" means that less processing is required to extract the nutrients. For example, cows and other ruminants eat grass and have multiple stomachs or large reticulum's to process the grass—the lowest quality food. Ruminants extract nutrients from grasses by a process called

---

17   https://www.journals.uchicago.edu/doi/10.1086/204350.

18   https://www.britannica.com/science/human-evolution/ Increasing-brain-size.

fermentation—the same process used to make alcohol. We, by contrast, have very small intestinal processing systems with a very limited ability to process via fermentation. Our gut uses acid to extract nutrients. This leads to the logical conclusion that our bodies evolved to need different nutrients than ruminants.

In contrast to plants, meat is much more nutrient-dense. Our brains allowed us to develop ways to improve the digestion of meat. Cooking pre-digests meat and removes toxins and microbes. Curing and smoking meats are methods our large brain developed to protect us against bacteria.

Our pancreas is also relatively small and evolved to handle low glycemic loads. Plants are the primary source of these glycemic loads. Through most of our evolutionary history, our bodies experienced low glycemic loads.

In evolutionary terms, if we compress 2.4 million years of human evolution into the 24 hours of a clock:

- We've been eating meat for 24 hours.
- We've been eating wheat for 6 minutes.
- We've been eating ultra-processed food for 4 seconds.

Our bodies have had relatively little time to adapt to grains, much less processed food.

Another way to look at the subject of health is to observe the results of a certain dietary lifestyle. The US Department of Agriculture (USDA) published a Food Pyramid several decades ago:

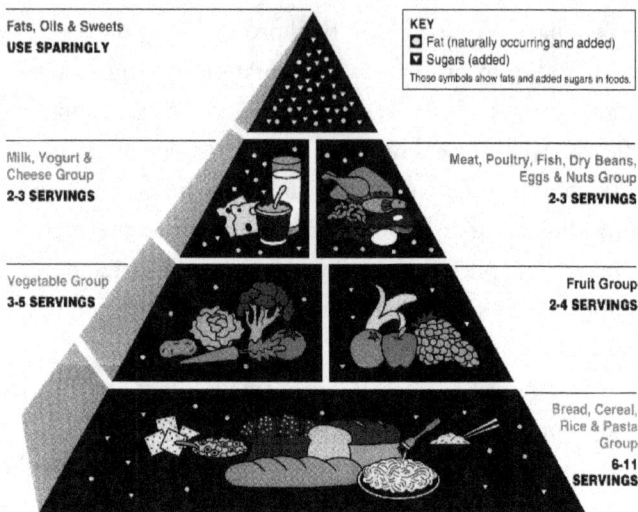

The USDA Food Pyramid recommended very little fat and protein in our diet and huge amounts of carbohydrates. Yet, our bodies don't need carbohydrates since our liver can make glucose. Our bodies cannot make fat or protein and need both from external sources.

- There are essential amino acids.
- There are essential fatty acids.
- There are no essential carbohydrates, yet the USDA recommends over 60 percent of caloric intake is carbohydrates!

After five decades of consuming the Standard American Diet, the results are clear. America has the highest rate of obesity in the developed world. According to the US Center for Disease Control (CDC) over 71 percent of Americans are overweight and 40 percent of these are obese. It is estimated that 85 percent of the adult population has metabolic syndrome, which is the current name for insulin resistance[19]. US cancer rates and heart disease are also at the top of the charts compared to other countries.

Those are pretty poor results from following the USDA's recommended diet! If you have health problems from eating improperly, government regulators were incorrect and it's time to seek the truth. Was the Food Pyramid a conspiracy designed to sicken US citizens? I think there is a more mundane explanation I'll cover in Chapter 39.

In the chemical plants where I worked, we were often asked to raise production rates as the market demand increased. The engineers searched for the bottlenecks—equipment that was limiting how fast we could run the line.

Our bodies have a bottleneck as well and that is the pancreas. Insulin is a hormone, and something called the insulin growth factor (IGF) is responsible for how big we become. Our brain seeks to increase growth by finding food that increases IGF. It's not surprising that our brain wants us to eat lots of carbohydrates. Carbs are cheap energy and a prime directive of the brain is energy conservation.Over time, however, our brains have evolved to create growth food faster than our pancreases have evolved to absorb the sugars. Our bodies cannot store much glucose, and, as a result, excess sugars are turned to fat. Our blood can carry only about a teaspoon of glucose. The excess sugar circulating in our bloodstream constantly signals the pancreas to produce more insulin. This creates a feedback loop that attempts to stabilize blood sugar levels. Every cell in our body has a receptor for insulin. Over time these cells become resistant to the excess insulin if there is a constant overload of carbohydrates. The graph below is a simulation of how one's insulin levels can swing up and down when regularly eating high glucose meals versus low glucose meals. The higher highs, as well as the higher average level of insulin over

---

19   *Why We Get Sick*, Dr. Benjamin Bikman

time, shuts down the insulin receptors in our cells. Consequently higher levels of insulin are needed to maintain constant glucose levels in our blood.

Insulin levels

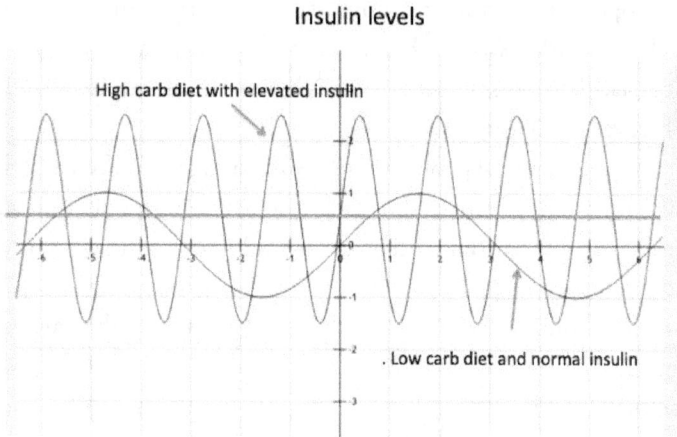

High carb diet with elevated insulin

Low carb diet and normal insulin

In the eighties, nutritionists advised that we should "graze" continuously between meals. Of course, this keeps the pancreas injecting insulin into our bodies around the clock. It is not at all what our ancestors did.

Elevated levels of insulin increase the amount of cortisol in our bodies, which puts us on edge and stimulates the fight, flight, fawn, or freeze response. I sometimes wonder if that is why there is so much tension in the US. I recall often being "hangry" (both angry and hungry) by the end of the workday to the point where I could not think clearly. That it is due to the swings in insulin levels as depicted in the chart above.

Many people today push plant-based diets as a healthy alternative or as a way to stop climate change. Based on the expensive tissue hypothesis, however, it is obvious that evolution directs us in the opposite direction.

Over 80% of the earth's land is only suitable for grasses to grow. Grass is the most abundant carbohydrate on the planet and ruminants have the perfect machinery to convert these carbs to fat and protein. Humans have evolved to extract the high-density nutrients from the ruminants with our acid-based digestion. That appears to be the perfect symbiosis.

This chart compares two different types of diets:

Plant-Based-Diet (PBD) versus Animal-Sourced-Food-Diet (ASFD)

PBD – low-quality diet	ASFD – high-quality diet
Deficient in key nutrients	Complete amino acid complement
Lacking complete protein	Bile can extract B-12
Lacking essential fatty acids	Volumetrically dense
Need to eat large volumes	Energy-dense
Requires fermentation	Nutrient-dense
Longer eating times	Provides essential fatty acids (EPA, DHA)
Higher intake of toxins	Lower processing requirement
	Reduced eating time

It is interesting to observe that those who are pushing PBDs also seem opposed to capitalism. Without the free enterprise system, those on a PBD would spend most of their days foraging for food. At the end of the day, they would still lack essential nutrients that plants cannot provide, such as vitamin B-12, essential fatty acids, and taurine.

Most people on some kind of vegetarian or vegan diet rely on processed foods to reduce the eating time and get sufficient calories. It takes a lot longer for someone eating plant-based foods to ingest enough food to survive, which is why vegetarians are usually lean. The likely result is that plant eaters end up consuming processed carbohydrates to make up that difference. Because of this many plant eaters, though thin, end up with fatty deposits on their livers due to constantly high insulin levels.[20] Processed foods deliver a very high glycemic load to our pancreas.

Science tells us that hyperinsulinemia produced by high glycemic load over time leads to insulin resistance. Many scientists hypothesize that insulin resistance is the predecessor to the major killers of our age: diabetes, cardiovascular disease, cancer, and dementia. Scientists have discovered that the brains of Alzheimer's victims are insulin resistant. Insulin resistance is why diets often don't work.

Another observation from the ancient past is that food wasn't always readily available. Prehistoric homo sapiens did not eat three meals per day much less graze. Our ancestor's bodies underwent the stress of not eating on a regular basis and the stress of exercising regularly in the search for food. The name for this process is hormesis, which I covered in Chapter 21. We stress our body but not enough to kill it. During this stress, our cells go through a process called autophagy where all the garbage in the cell is recycled for new purposes. Without initiating autophagy, junk can accumulate in our cells, which many scientists believe causes inflammation. Inflammation has been linked to cancer and heart disease.

Modern scientists have discovered that the practice of caloric restriction is the one proven method of extending our lifespan. Nature wants to give us more time to reproduce when times are lean.

---

20 · Diabetes is a major problem in India in low weight individuals despite vegetarian diets.

The graph below shows a look at how long it takes for insulin levels in our blood to drop in response to shutting down the pancreas. Giving the pancreas a break improves insulin sensitivity and decreases insulin resistance. It takes eighteen to twenty-four hours to get rid of 80 percent of the insulin in our blood.[21]

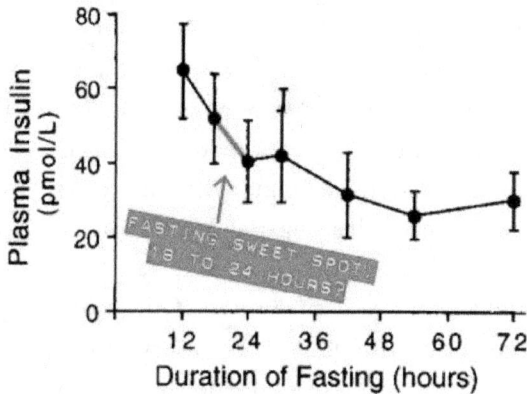

I've tested this with a ketone meter and found it to be quite close to my experience. Blood ketones increase as insulin levels decrease, so it is a good proxy for insulin. Exercise also drops insulin levels, and exercise during a fast compounds that affect.

The USDA has replaced the food pyramid with their "MyPlate" app, which proffers essentially the same proportions of carbs, fats and proteins with a slick marketing campaign. The USDA hopes that substituting refined grains with more carbohydrates from vegetables and fruits will stem the tide of obesity and disease. The same financial interests are behind this modified look and it's another experiment being run by the government with no scientific basis.

The USDA also pushes polyunsaturated fats over animal fats

---

21   https://www.ncbi.nlm.nih.gov/pubmed/8238506

as "heart healthy." Most of these oils are plant-based seed oils processed at high temperatures. High temperatures produce oxidized fats. Oxidation is linked to inflammation. Several studies have linked the consumption of these oils with insulin resistance.[22] Dr. Michael Eades makes a compelling hypothesis that linoleic acid from seed oils actually changes the way our cell mitochondria produce ATP.[23] These oils actually make our fat (adipose) cells larger and the pathway that signals satiety is higher. In other words, we have to eat more to feel full. Seed oils are high in omega-6 fatty acids, which cause an inflammatory response in our cells[24]. The use of seed oils is rampant in processed food and their introduction to the human diet is only one hundred twenty years. Processed food contains refined grains, sugar and seed oils, and increased consumption correlates with obesity and disease.

A final thought in regards to nutrition. Our evolutionary drive is to grow and become strong in order to survive and reproduce. We need lots of energy in our first three decades to grow our bodies and brain. For hundreds of thousands of years, once we've reached about thirty years old, we have stopped growing and completed our reproductive mission. Continuing to eat a carbohydrate-filled diet after our metabolism has stopped growing leads to problems. The body has no place to store the extra glucose. We cannot eat what our children eat. The one strategy that has increased the lifespan and health of mammals is caloric restriction after the growth phase is completed.

So what can we learn from looking at our bodies from an evolutionary perspective?

---

22   https://www.researchgate.net/publication/269696521_A_high_fat_diet_
rich_in_corn_oil_reduces_spontaneous_locomotor_activity_and_induces_
insulin_resistance_in_mice

23   https://proteinpower.com/a-new-hypothesis-of-obesity/.

24   https://pubmed.ncbi.nlm.nih.gov/22570770/

- Pre-digested, nutrient-dense animal-sourced food is more likely to provide our brains with the energy it needs than a raw or plant-based diet.

- Our digestive system uses acid not fermentation to break down food. It is designed to break down fats and proteins and extract vital nutrients from meats not large quantities of plant foods.Highly processed modern food has a high glycemic load, which our pancreas cannot handle. The response, over time, is insulin resistance, which leads to disease.

- Our brain seeks more carbohydrates than our bodies can handle. It may take millennia for our bodies to catch up with our ability to manufacture cheap carbs, and so self-discipline is needed in our eating behavior.

- The body needs periods of high stress loads, exercise, and fasting to clean out the garbage in its cells.

It is quite interesting that all the major religions advocate a fasting regimen. Was there some ancient understanding of the need to stress the body with no food? Science is only now catching up to this wisdom.

Just as our stories control results we get in life, the food we eat produces results in both our health and lifespan. Pretending that our bodies are out of our control and only a doctor can fix us with a pill leads to much pain and suffering.

In our second year living in our RV, my wife and I were out mountain biking in California. I felt really good and was taking chances. Unfortunately, one of those led to a fall and a broken hip. At the hospital, doctors informed me that 50 percent of people over sixty who break a hip die within six months and 90 percent of the rest are permanently disabled. I had been biking in the high elevations of Colorado all summer and eating well. I was not a typical sixty-two-year-old. I was told I would not be able to bike for six months and ski for at least a year. Eight weeks after the surgery I got on my bike. I skied a couple of months later. A year later, no one would know I broke a hip. The doctors told me how unusual a patient I was. Was it good genes or a good lifestyle that was responsible for this recovery?

Figure 1.

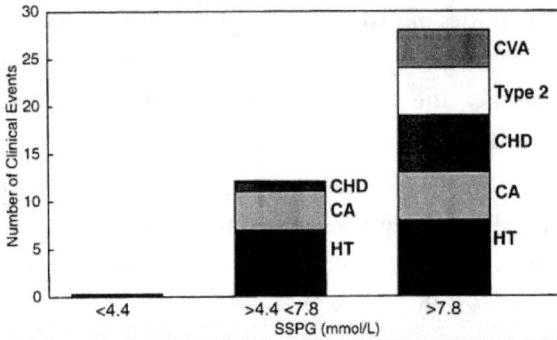

I'll leave this subject with one more chart.[25] A Stanford University study looked at steady-state plasma glucose (SSPG) levels of 208 individuals in their forties with no evidence of disease. The SSPG test is a measure of insulin resistance. At the end of the study (an average of six years later), health events measured were: hypertension (HT), cancer (CA), diabetes (Type 2), coronary heart disease (CHD) and cerebrovascular accident (CVA).

∽

None of the study participants in the group with the best insulin sensitivity had an event. Nearly one-fifth of those at high insulin levels developed a serious disease and three died. Diabetes, cardiovascular disease, cancer, and hypertension were all associated with high insulin resistance. It's clear that the results of a high carbohydrate intake are deadly.

---

25 · https://academic.oup.com/jcem/article/86/8/3574/2848584.

The expensive tissue hypothesis allows us to view our health from the viewpoint of our brains. I spent a lot of time on this section because I have seen firsthand how poor nutrition impacts decision-making in people close to me. Having a clear mind is the key to executing the high-level ideas in this book. Don't eat to save the planet. Eat to save your brain, and it will develop ways to save the planet.

There are two essential tools that everyone can use to remake their health:

1. A tool for insulin control is tracking HOMA-IR. Homeostatic Model of Assessment for Insulin Resistance is a simple formula. It is the product of fasting glucose times fasting insulin divided by 405. Higher HOMA-IR ratios strongly correlate with poor health.[26] A ratio below 1.2 is considered insulin sensitive. Continuous glucose monitors are great tools to assess which foods cause your glucose to spike. I highly recommend getting one for a two-week test and figure out what foods work best for keeping your glucose levels under control. If you need a prescription, there are telemedicine sites available to acquire one.

2. Get a heart rate variability (HRV) monitor. HRV is a measure of the variation between heartbeats. It sounds counter-intuitive but the higher your HRV (the less consistent your heartbeats are), the healthier you are. Tracking your HRV can tell you about your level of fitness, alert you to an illness days before you feel symptoms, and help you to reduce your stress levels. HRV trends can also predict more serious illnesses like diabetes or heart disease.

---

26   https://cebp.aacrjournals.org/content/29/1/157.abstract.

31

STAYING CONTENT

KEEPING UP WITH the Joneses is an old saying that refers to trying to keep up with the material largess of one's neighbor. The accumulation of material goods was used as a social status benchmark of success.

Today, social media gives us the means to compare ourselves to not just our neighbors but to every successful person on the planet. Marketing departments of all successful companies know which buttons to push to trigger us to want something that we currently don't have. It's no wonder that dissatisfaction is so rampant throughout society and contentment is so hard to find.

The fruit of dissatisfaction is unhappiness. Dissatisfaction, though, is not entirely bad. Dissatisfaction can lead to two different paths depending on the story you create about it. The most common path is envy and jealousy that creates a desire to drag those with more than us down to our level. The root of this type of dissatisfaction is the storyline of victimhood. Punishing others because we view them as stealing the wealth, which oppresses us in some way, is the evil behavior that Dostoevsky wrote about.

Just because someone has more than us doesn't mean we should hope that they suffer.

The second type of story that people create out of dissatisfaction is a desire to create solutions to the perceived problem. For example, figuring out how to make more money so we can buy a home like our neighbors. Or maybe we create a new drug to cure a deadly virus we fear or a diet that solves our dissatisfaction with our health.

All the great advancements that allow us to live comfortable, safe, and long lives were born of dissatisfaction with the way things were that led to a desire to solve the problem.

The key to reducing unhappiness is to recognize the source of our discomfort and decide what to do. The Debugging Software is a great tool for this.

We have to be honest about the root of our dissatisfaction. Are we just complaining or are we willing to work to find a solution?

Being able to recognize if social status envy, good marketing, or childhood trauma is the root of our triggers can give us an aha moment. This can liberate us to be content with what we have. And if we can turn dissatisfaction into desire and solve a real problem that people have, we won't be afraid to be temporarily unhappy in pursuit of our mission.

It is also important to recognize that we do not have to submit to the efforts of marketing gurus when they try to persuade us that we need that new car, designer clothes, or cruise to Bali. Instead, we can choose to be content with what we have.

Think of being content as the heat sink[27] in our computer. It dissipates all the heat generated by excessive program executions.

Being content means being grateful for what we have. It means

---

27   Computer chips generate lots of heat while running computations. The heat must be removed or the chip will fail quickly. A heat sink is usually a large piece of metal that radiates the heat away.

having the story that "I am enough." It means not holding any grievances. It mostly means not playing the victim. When triggers occur, we let them go. We enjoy the work we do for no reason but to improve the world. We enjoy and accept the people we interact with without judgment.

This may seem at odds with my earlier suggestion that we need to have goals, but the answer lies in the root of the trigger. If the trigger creates dissatisfaction that is all about us and our Me story, we will not find contentment. When the desire becomes the satisfaction of exploring the chaos and expanding our sense of who we are, then we will find great contentment in that desire. Contentment comes in our personal path of growth, not in anything external.

32

STAYING
OPPORTUNITY FOCUSED

Is YOUR JOB drudgery? Are you full of anxiety Sunday evening knowing the next day starts another week kowtowing to a boss you dislike? Do you long for the freedom to be on your own living on a farm in nature?

First, think about your boss. Is he or she inept, an ogre, or dismissive of your accomplishments? Unless you quit your job you may think you are stuck.

I thought this way for many years. I lived for the weekend. I tried to drown the drudgery with lots of beer and even marijuana to escape from what I thought was the drudgery of the grind.

Using the Debugging Software I reframed my thinking to look at work as an opportunity, even when I hated it.

Recognize that your boss is mostly interested in one thing—him or herself. Period. Everything that they do—even if it is expressing an interest in you—is designed to help them. In my first management role, I told myself it was my job to fix my boss. I judged he had made some ethical errors, so I ratted him out to his boss. That led to an embarrassing demotion. In retrospect, I see that one of an employee's primary jobs is to make his or her boss look good. That is more likely to get you the promotion you desire. This will also feed our innate desire to feel important.

I learned this late in my career. As a result, in two of the last three years of my career, I received a corporate Engineering Excellence award. A sharp contrast with the demotion I received thirty-five years earlier when I was such a smart ass!

A second way to reframe our job is to look at it as a paid learning experience. Someone else is paying us to gain the confidence and skills to move to another job or to start our own business. We can learn the skills of what we do on a day-to-day basis better by acquiring new knowledge through seminars or schools and even insights from the Internet.

We can also study the company's financials, if they are public, observe its marketing strategies, its HR policies, and any number of business-related matters. This will provide us with a much greater perspective on how to be more valuable to our current employer as well as educate us about how a business should be managed. If we make our job a game to be mastered rather than a chore, then we may start to look forward to Monday mornings with anticipation rather than dread.

The Internet provides a bottomless resource of opportunities to learn new skills. Scott Adams in his book *How to Fail at Almost Everything and Still Win Big* promotes developing a "talent stack," which means layering multiple skills on top of each other to give yourself a very unique skill set.

The Internet can also provide limitless markets for us to offer our skill set to the world. Some marketplaces like Upwork.com help us expose our value to millions of potential buyers. I've found excellent talent from around the world on Upwork.com. There is a tremendous free market aspect of Upwork. As your reputation grows, you are rewarded much more than an average person with the same credentials.

There is no reason to be a slave to our job if we have a desire to create a new story about work.

You may wonder why I, an engineer working for a large corporation, told the story of sitting in a room in New York City with a group of entrepreneurs. The genesis of that story goes back to my time in Amway decades earlier. While I did not make lots of money while part of Amway, I did learn some valuable lessons. One of the most important lessons was to be a life-long student.

As a result, I invested and continue to invest lots of money on books and courses to explore new areas and learn new skills, like marketing and sales. As I write this book I am investing in writing courses. These skills helped me to be a better employee as well as to understand business and entrepreneurship.

I'll discuss this more in Chapter 42 on educational risk taking.

33
STAYING CONFIDENT

THE RESULTS WE get in life are often less about our qualifications and more about our confidence. Activities like getting a job, making the sale, getting a date, mastering a skill, or winning a game most of the time boil down to being or acting confident.

The difference between being confident and acting confident is one of the stories we tell ourselves.

My first job after graduating from college was with DuPont in West Virginia. They hired about thirty engineers around the same time. The newly hired engineers and I would hang out together after work hours. One new engineer would take colleagues flying on weekends and tell stories of his escapades as a white water rafting guide. After several months he was fired when HR discovered he didn't have an engineering degree.

It turned out that he didn't have a pilot's license either!

He was a con man, as in CONfidence.

His confidence helped him to do things he was never trained to do. He was probably a good pilot. Still, I'm glad I never got in a plane with him!

I've also sat across from brilliantly qualified engineers interviewing for jobs who had so little self-confidence they could not look me in the eye. And they did not get hired despite their qualifications and IQ.

Many self-help books suggest that we act as if we were already successful. The truth is that most of the confident people we admire were often scared or uncertain when they started. But they saw themselves as successful and expected to get the result they wanted.

The opposite of people with confidence is those that acquiesce to others all the time. Instead of creating their own stories, they live in other people's stories much like Walter Mitty. Unconfident people are bit actors instead of a leading man or woman. Those people that just go along to get along rarely get what they want. They are exhibiting the fawn response to fear.

There are two types of confidence:

- Confidence in performing a skill.
- Confidence when dealing with people.

To attack this frame we need to go into the Debugging Software and understand our Me stories. For the skill-based issues, the surest bet of where the bugs are is in the "I am" stories: I am clumsy, I am not smart enough, I am too old to learn, I am too young, and so on. Unsure people tell themselves these stories out of a fear of the unknown and fear of what other people think.

As children, many of us read or heard the book *The Little Engine That Could*. There was a little engine who helped bring the train cars into the railyard but never went over the big hill to the town on the other side. One day an engine pulling cars full of food and toys breaks down. The little engine asks several larger engines to help take the cars to the town so the boys and girls can have good things to eat and toys to play with. They all refuse, so the little engine takes on the task himself. As he struggles to get over the hill he repeats to himself, "I think I can. I think I can. I think I can" I told myself that exact phrase when climbing the last mile up Pikes Peak on my bike when the tour operator told me to stop. If that phrase triggers us, we need to explore our Me stories and figure out why.

Regarding the second type of confidence, dealing with other people, this is often an intimidation issue that we absorb as our story. In ancient times this fear came from a fear that the more powerful person would physically harm us. Now the fear is a social status construct. It is an internal story that the other person is more powerful than us and might expose and humiliate us. Or the unsure person might worry about what the other person is thinking of us.

One of the things I am grateful for in my experience with Amway was that it forced me to gain confidence in speaking with people. First, I had to speak with one or two people at a kitchen table to convince them to host an event. Then I had to speak to groups of four to ten people with a whiteboard. The leader in the business told us to dress sharply in a suit and tie when speaking with groups to gain confidence, and it worked.

As our networking business grew, I got to speak in front of groups of twenty to fifty people. Eventually, I ended up speaking to crowds of three thousand to five thousand people and loved doing it. I thoroughly enjoyed expanding my being.

One of the strategies for dealing with the fear of others is alluded to in the famous book *Dress for Success* by John T. Moyer. When you look sharper than others, you create a story that says you are more successful and thus more powerful, which in turn drives the emotion of self-confidence. Clothing feeds our story of superior social status.

Another strategy is to speak louder than normal when you feel intimidated by others. Most of the time when we are intimidated, we tend to speak softer than normal. Speaking louder actually creates self-confidence. The story you are telling yourself is that you are important and deserve to be heard.

Once we sort out our Me stories about why we feel intimidated, feeling confident is a skill we can develop just like playing tennis. We can also search for shortcuts or hacks, like the two examples above, to trick ourselves into being more confident.

It is easy to create confidence when we perceive we have higher social status. Tricking our brains into that mode when we lack confidence can help us gain faith in ourselves.

Life is so short. Do you want to live in someone else's story and help them get what they want? Or do you want to adopt a frame of confidence so you will get yourself further in life?

34

STAYING SEXY

Maslow's Pyramid shows sex at the base. Our mating instinct is nearly as strong as our will to survive. If we view the world through the frame of mating, most of our stories, emotions, and actions revolve around sex. Most of our social climbing and preening has to do with finding mates. Our willingness to work beyond what is essential for survival is often motivated by the desire to appeal to the opposite sex. I've watched TV awards shows with the most ardent feminists dressed to the nines to enhance their sexual desirability. Since mating is so vital to our species, paying attention to what we think and tell ourselves about sex is critical to our happiness and well-being.

What do you think about your sexuality? Our cultural mores and tribal influences in our life play a massive role in the stories we create about sex. In most civilized countries there appear to be morals that inhibit certain sexual interactions. These unwritten codes of conduct were most likely initiated to protect against pregnancy and disease or jealousy and murder. There may have been mutual compacts of willingness to provide sex in exchange for protection. In more recent times a case can be made that they were also designed to protect our hearts from rejection.

The prevailing structure for male-female relationships in most of the world is monogamy. Religious groups are especially influential in governing sexual behavior. Many in the West blame Christianity as the reason for this, but my wife grew up in China and the sexual taboos she learned in an atheist/Buddhist society were much stricter than any we experience in the West today. So sexual mores are pretty universal.

What humans learn and absorb in childhood plays a huge role in how we think and live as adults. How our parents viewed sexuality impacts us tremendously. Even after following the rules and getting married, people can struggle with their sexuality because of childhood influences. If you were taught that a sex act is wrong for years, it is very difficult to unlearn that thinking. But that is the purpose of this book—to reexamine what we learned in our youth. What we learned may or may not be useful to us as an adult, but if we are not getting the results we want, then it is time to reconsider the old stories.

So if sex triggers us, here are some things to evaluate with the Debugging Software:

- Do I have "I am" stories around my body appearance?
- Am I "mind reading" my partner's thoughts during sex?
- Am I too absorbed in myself that I am more worried about my performance than the pleasure of my partner?
- Am I open to experimentation or is there only one correct way to be sexual? This is a chaos vs. order modality to be discussed in Chapter 40.
- If something goes badly during sex and I am triggered, what are the Me stories?

At the beginning of Part V, I made a list of all the tribes that influence me. Do this for yourself and assess what impact each has on your current beliefs and stories around sex. Then evaluate if it is useful to you to maintain those beliefs.

Sex exposes us in more than the physical nakedness of it. It exposes who we are and makes it difficult for us to hide our flaws. Good sex is quite chaotic. However, if we have too many hang-ups, we try to make it routine and orderly. When sex becomes mechanical it ceases to be exciting.

Nature has contrived to make sex one of the most physically and emotionally rewarding experiences that humans engage in. If we are not getting that, it's worth evaluating our scripts and stories about it.

I don't have all the answers about this topic, and it's a huge area occupying the base of Maslow's hierarchy. Consider if your framework and the stories you tell yourself are getting you the results you want both short term and long term. If not, reconsider your beliefs about sex.

35

GROWING UP

THE PARENT-CHILD RELATIONSHIP is the strongest frame we use to shape our stories, as the family is the most important tribal group. The first years of our life are usually spent with parents and those years imprint deeply into our psyche.

Sadly, many people go through their adult life still acting as a child whenever there is an interaction with a parent. The main obstacle to continuing with a parent-child relationship into adulthood is that this relationship is often based on an oppressor-victim frame. The parent acts with power still giving out advice as an order, and the child acts powerless, unable to contradict or make a case for their own ideas. When we become adults these issues impact the wife-husband relationship, how we raise our children, financial decisions, and even where we live.

It is important to be grateful to our parents for giving us life and, if they raised us, for all the sacrifices they made supporting us. And it's also good to give them respect if they have earned it.

But as an adult, it is more valuable for us to have a more mature relationship with our parents. Parents can be resources to help us understand our childhood and sometimes come to our help later in life. I remember both sets of parents coming to our aid during a family crisis after adopting four children from Russia. I don't recall exactly when it happened, but over time all of my siblings and I started calling our parents by their first names. Sure, we still occasionally called them Mom and Dad, but routinely we would use their first names just like two adults talking to each other.

This reminds both parties that there is no longer a parent-child or dominant-submissive relationship. It frees us in our mind from old stories of control or neediness.

Just like we saw in Chapter 29 on finding independence the parent-child relationship can be based on neediness. Both parent and child can crave the attention and love of the other.

If we are a parent who looks at their child as a validation of our parent skills, we may have an inclination to control them. Part of that may be creating expectations around family gatherings after our children become teens and then adults.

As an example, it is very common to see young families torn between the two different sets of parents demanding they attend a family gathering during major holidays. Both sets of in-laws might try to exert control, which causes stress in their adult children.

Growing up means letting our adult children go their own way.

Growing up means we can respect our parents and not be obligated to them. True, they spent lots of energy and love raising you. That does not mean that we are required to please them. Growing up means making our own decisions about what is best for us.

Growing up is about throwing away the childhood stories that were programmed into us and creating our own new stories. It's time to recognize that our parents did the best job they could with the skills and level of consciousness they possessed. They may not have been the parents we wanted, but they were the parents we needed to become the person we are today.

Be grateful and have respect for your parents. Then create your own life stories.

36

GETTING OUTSIDE YOUR EGO

IF YOU'VE EVER read any books on sales skills, the first thing you learn is that the person you are trying to sell to is only thinking about one thing: him or herself.

This is true in everything, not just sales. That is why the Debugging Software suggests looking at the opposite view. Most people spend 95 percent of their time absorbed in their own problems. When we feel triggered by what someone else does or says, they probably weren't even thinking of us. They most likely were stuck on themselves.

As I discussed back in the beginning of this book, our initial state of being in the world is self-absorption. Everything we see we interpret to be about us. We develop strong stories of the world being against us. Sometimes these stories devolve into conspiracy theories to buttress our belief in our victim status.

Getting outside that mind frame can be a struggle. However, there is one sure antidote: service to others.

Serving others gets us away from being constantly focused on our problems. As we have learned, our problems usually trigger many of our stories. Serving others without seeking attention for our efforts provides an internal boost in self-esteem. It creates an "I am a good person" story. When we try to create a story based on getting praise from others for our good works, however, it creates an "I am a hypocrite" story. Remember that we have a strong tendency for attention-seeking. It's important to be real to get the benefits of serving others.

In some ways serving others is actually like meditation. When we are focused on others, it disrupts that stream of self-absorbed thoughts that are constantly triggering us.

Serving others doesn't necessarily mean we need to sell all our belongings and join Mother Teresa's nunnery in India. There are many people in our life whom we can serve. If we are in a relationship, we can start by serving our partner. This means helping them without expecting something in return. Too often we will do something in a relationship with the expectation of a quid pro quo. One of the persuasion techniques that author Robert Cialdini writes of is called reciprocity. When we do something for others, we expect that they will do something for us. That is why Hare Krishna handed out brochures or Costco hands out free food samples. When we do something without expecting anything in return, it is surprising and perceived as a loving act. It spreads good into the world.

If we are employees we can serve our company or our boss by making them look good. If we don't like our boss, help them get a promotion so they will "move on." If we are in a position where we interact with customers, we can make sure that they have the best experience possible in our retail business rather than thinking about what time we get off work.

There are little ways we can also serve our fellow humans in everyday life. Acts like holding the door open or giving up our seat on the subway or even helping an elderly person cross the street all return benefits to us.

During my many "lake effect" snowstorms in the Buffalo, New York area, I'd experience three or four feet of snow being dumped on us. Neighbors would help each other by shoveling walkways and driveways or bringing meals to elderly folks on the street.

We put our self-absorbed ego aside when we are in a constant state of service. I think this is the antidote to Dostoevsky's thesis about our collective responsibility for the evil in the world. We are all responsible for the good in the world and service to others is the manifestation of that good. We have an obligation to understand and empathize with others to sow good on the world.

37
STAYING CONNECTED

"Equations are us"

—Dr. James Gates

I'VE MENTIONED DOSTOEVSKY'S idea that we are all responsible for all the bad in the world. If we see ourselves as distinct and disconnected from others, his idea is a hard concept to accept.

It's easy to see other people and creatures as distinct from us. In the US there is a strong culture of individualism, which promotes an "us" versus "them" mind frame for our stories. The "connected" versus "individual" frames are one of reality's dualities. Both exist simultaneously.

One of the reasons as a scientist I cannot be an atheist is the awe I experience anytime a new scientific discovery is made. The universe seems to be made with extreme mathematical precision. In quantum mechanics, for example, scientists keep finding layer after layer of new particles inside accelerators where atoms are crashed into each other at near the speed of light.

Particle physicists tell us that we actually are quite connected. In school, we learned to understand that our bodies are composed of atoms made up of electrons spinning around some protons. But at the quantum level, the story is bizarre. Those particles break down into smaller and smaller particles and then disappear into energy patterns. And when scientists try to measure the location of those particles, they are not in an exact place. Their location falls along a curve of probabilities!

So when you look at someone, you are looking at energy patterns. The air that separates us is also an energy pattern, so there is a continuum of energy patterns between what I think I am and what I think someone else is. What distinguishes someone else's energy patterns from our energy patterns is not well established.

Scientists who study the related field of science called chaos theory postulate a so-called butterfly effect. Small changes in the initial state of a system result in large changes downstream. A simple expression of this complex idea is that when a butterfly flaps its wings in one part of the world the effect is felt halfway around the world with the potential to create a hurricane.

In practical terms, what this means is that every action you take has numerous and large effects over time that are unpredictable. And one of the strangest theories of quantum mechanics is Bell's theorem. John Bell was a physicist who showed that every observer affects what is being observed and that effect transcends space and time. We affect the probability patterns of the space we observe.

In practical terms what this means is that the world we are seeing is a direct result of what we are paying attention to. This involves complex quantum physics phenomena called entanglement. Since we are "entangled" at a quantum level, this solidifies the idea that we are all very well connected. What we do affects others around us now and in the future. Think of how my act of leaving home as a teen influenced my siblings fifty years ago.

When I first discussed reality in Chapter 11, I noted that what we observe with our senses acts as a user interface. We are familiar with this concept from interacting with the computer desktop. We know that a file icon is not really a file but a series of zeros and ones in a transistor. Likewise, our senses are interpreting subatomic energy vibrations that we don't understand and indicating to us what is safe and what is not. We don't have the tools to understand the code making up our existence. But we know that we can manipulate it much like John Bell postulated.

When we consider the ideas of energy, the butterfly effect, and entanglement, it is quite likely that we are all connected in some way.

When I integrated these physics concepts with Dostoevsky's ideas, it made perfect sense. Our stories are integral to all that is going on in the world. It's quite possible to imagine that when we get angry in New York, someone in Tokyo will feel the effects at some point. Particle properties are the closest insight we have as to how connected we really are.

If we see the actions we take as only important to us right now, then we ignore what may be more significant long term. We also discount our value to the world.

The best representation of how this may work is the movie *Groundhog Day* starring Bill Murray as Phil Conner. In the movie, Phil wakes up every morning, and it is the same day. Phil is very self-absorbed and sees himself as the center of the universe. But Phil takes different actions every day, and the results of his actions have a large effect over time on the people around him.

In the end, Phil recognizes that he is connected to all the people with whom he interacts. Even the smallest interactions make a huge difference to some. By accepting this connectedness, Phil becomes profoundly loved by all the people in the town. It's a very profound movie, and I highly recommend watching it multiple times.

The connectedness mind frame allows us to feel more empathy for our fellow humans. When we see ourselves as distinct, we often fear the other and have no empathy. When we see ourselves as connected to others, it makes it much more difficult for us to inflict pain on them and to be willing to understand the pain they may be experiencing.

This is why serving others has so much power in helping us grow. By serving others you are serving what you are connected to. You are actually serving yourself.

See yourself as connected to others, and you can create many new stories about love and empathy instead of fear and anger.

38
STAYING GRATEFUL

ONE GREAT FRAMEWORK that we can embrace that produces much joy is to adopt a gratitude story. Many people view the world with bitterness, envy, and jealousy. They see themselves as victims of the system and powerless to do anything about their lives.

Many times people who are ungrateful spend time comparing themselves to those they feel have better lives. This is social status envy. An ingratitude story will bring on much unhappiness in your life. Instead, you should reframe your story to see everything in your life as a gift. You can be grateful you were born in the twentieth or twenty-first century rather than two hundred or one thousand years ago when life was nasty, brutish, and short. You can be grateful for your family, even if your time with them was traumatic.

"How?" You may ask.

By looking at the lessons you have learned from your experiences. Think about how those experiences have helped you grow. And then you need to forgive those who have hurt you. Forgiveness is simply having empathy for someone else's state of consciousness at that time and recognizing their actions were what they were capable of at that moment in time. You can also be grateful your parents gave birth to you. That whole birthing thing was not the most pleasant for our mothers.

One of the current trends in social media is to dig into a person's past and crucify them for their behavior when they were younger. It's called the "cancel" culture. This cancel culture assumes that this person should have known better at that earlier age.

Instead, we should view people as having made the best decisions and had the best behavior possible for them at the age the supposed transgression occurred. And then forgive them for their infractions of our moral canons. We often use phrases like "You could have" or "You should have" to insinuate that the other person had the capability that we have to act differently. The reality is that they could not have without a different consciousness.

I remember at one point I was finally able to see my parents from their viewpoint. I saw how they learned from their parents who had learned from their parents all the way back to the beginning of their lineage. I saw how they struggled to make money and support their children. I recognized that they had internal stories about being victims, which created anger. That anger which I thought was directed at me was really due to something else. At that moment I had complete empathy for them and was able to totally forgive them for how they had raised me.

I looked at my childhood experiences in a whole new light.

Having a grateful attitude involves framing our current life circumstances to see the good. We can look at the criticism of a parent as an attack or an opportunity to get better. We can see our job as drudgery or an opportunity to learn how to serve better. We can see disease as an opportunity to live a healthier life. We can see someone else's anger as an opportunity to have empathy and to encourage them.

We can choose to see every trigger as an unresolved personal issue. Be grateful that you were triggered and now have an opportunity to grow personally. Be grateful that the other person was around to make you aware of these unresolved issues. Imagine if you can say, "Thank you, for exposing an unresolved situation that I need to work on" when you have a bad interaction. Our triggers are not about what other people do to us; they are about us. What if just one of the two men in the road rage incident I mentioned earlier had thought, "I'm triggered and must have a personal issue around this. I'm grateful that dude cut me off." Two husbands and fathers would then be alive today.

Being grateful for everything is truly a marvelous approach to reaping happiness. Focus on what you have, not on a story of lack.

39

RELINQUISHING OUR URGE TO SAVE OTHERS

"The urge to save humanity is almost always a false-front for the urge to rule it. Power is what all messiahs really seek: not the chance to serve. This is true even of the pious brethren who carry the gospel to foreign parts."

—H.L. Mencken

WE'VE COVERED A lot so far, and you might be tempted to evangelize your new knowledge. Understand that you cannot save others. They can only save themselves, and they are unlikely to act until they are desperate for change.

Here is one thought to keep in mind when dealing with others:

I can be a leader and a teacher but not a savior.

We can teach people good strategies, but in the end, they have to save themselves.

Saviors fall into two categories:

1. The enablers who try to save people in order to satisfy some need for validation of their importance.
2. The tyrants who want to impose order on the world to give themselves power over others as well as to hide their fear.

Sometimes "helping" people enables them to remain powerless and continue to suffer. There are countless examples of do-gooders whose "charity" hurts the people they are supposedly helping.[28]

The more dangerous types of saviors are those who seek power and control. Forcing another to behave in a manner that they think is right is actually an impulse to control others.

You may read this and think of these types of saviors as the dictators of the world. However, many people are engaged in this type of saving on a more subtle level. For example, the world is full of evangelists of one type or another, who, in American journalist and cultural critic H. L. Mencken's words, are using their work as a false front to rule others.

I first encountered this while visiting Russia to adopt children. The host family constantly spied on us and ransacked our luggage when we were out of the apartment. The impulse to turn in neighbors for supposedly violating the "stay at home" rules in the US during the 2020 COVID-19 pandemic revealed that dark impulse in Americans.

If you think you are doing it for them, consider your Me story. Are you motivated to save others to feel important, get loved, gain attention, feel safe, or rule over others? If we are fearful and want

---

28 · Lyndon Johnson's "Great Society" program is one such example with regard to the African-American family. It incentivized out of wedlock pregnancy and fatherless families in exchange for free money in the name of reducing poverty but has had no effect on the poverty level and locked generations into increased crime and dependence.

to create more order to feel safe, it's a natural impulse to want to control others. In the COVID-19 crisis, those with the most fear of catching the disease were most likely to rat out people breaking quarantine rules. The behavior was unhinged from the reality on the ground.

A real savior does not believe they can change others by forcing their views on them. A good teacher leads the student to the water and lets them decide whether or not to drink.

Activism sometimes breaks down from an education process to a disruption/destruction process when the activists feel they are not being given enough recognition.

Jesus, Gandhi, and Martin Luther King Jr. were not interested in ruling in this world. They viewed themselves as teachers hoping to educate the world. We can tell by the long term results of their teachings that their mode of saving was much more effective than any dictator has ever been.

Dr. Jordan Peterson's dictum that "If you want to change the world, first clean your room" is relevant here. Often young people, who comprise the majority of most activist groups, are motivated by their fears of the unknown in the world as well as by their views about justice. Activism gives them a sense of purpose. Having a purpose should motivate us to improve our personal skills. I question whether protesting, engaging in property destruction, or violently confronting people is in the best interest of the activists. Personal growth cannot happen while destroying things, as that is just the rage of a victim.

It's hard to take rioters' demands seriously when they are destroying businesses. I would be much more open to an animal group introducing me to a cow than to those wearing anarchist masks. If we really want to save the world, our time is best spent on improving our own skills. The fear of the unknown drives much of the need to control others. Becoming competent reduces much of that fear.

It is also true that the people who really change the world are the leaders, not the marchers. A true leader does not impose his or her will on others. A real savior finds a solution to help people who he or she believes are oppressed. Seeking justice means helping the victim and not enabling them. Most people seeking justice, desire to punish the perceived oppressors.

When we believe we have to save someone, we should be very certain what consequences our actions will produce. Sometimes our actions enable more of the behavior we are supposed to be stopping. Sometimes our actions cause others to react negatively and more rebelliously. Sometimes our actions oppress others.

I remember Hare Krishna groups trying to shove pamphlets into my face at airports. It didn't move me to even read their papers much less join their religion.

Our desire to force others into our beliefs is quite an evil complex generated by our internal insecurities and lies at the heart of conflict. Relinquishing control indicates we are free of those inner struggles.

The table below shows some savior type tendencies and the ways to reframe each of them.

Belief	Current Practice	Better Options
Animals should be treated like humans and not eaten or abused.	Disrupting people's businesses and destroying their property.	Become a scientist to make delicious meat substitutes. Become an entrepreneur to market non-meat products.

You need to find Jesus to get to heaven.	Getting in people's faces about how they need to be saved.	Becoming a model citizen by living a moral life. Start a non-profit that demonstrates love for those in need by teaching the poor life skills.
Police are pigs.	Rioting and destroying property.	Become a policeman and work to change the system from within. Start a non-profit that teaches criminals life skills and correct thinking so that they get out of the crime business.

∽

The story of the origin of the USDA Food Pyramid, which was pushed decades ago recommended very little fat and protein in your diet and huge amounts of carbohydrates. Yet, our bodies don't need carbohydrates since our liver can make glucose. The pyramid was not a conspiracy theory. Neither was it based on science. Strangely, the justification for how we eat is based on religious activism and a vision from God.

Ellen G. White, a young woman with a history of seizures, claimed that visions during her seizures directed her to not eat meat. Shortly thereafter she was at the center of the founding of the Seventh Day Adventists (SDA). The SDA has focused on health and practiced vegetarianism since its inception. One of the early members was a young man named John Kellogg from Battle Creek Michigan. Kellogg became a doctor and started the Battle

Creek Sanitarium to further the church's mission. But Kellogg is most famous for the cereal company that bears his name.

Kellogg never consummated his marriage and was obsessed with sexual purity. In fact, he believed that corn flakes would prevent sexual stimulation and masturbation. Although he had some strange ideas on sex, Kellogg went on to found hospitals and colleges to train medical professionals in the meatless ways of the church. Another Adventist, Lenna Frances Cooper, founded the American Dietetic Association, which is now the Academy of Nutrition and Dietetics. This is the largest diet lobby group in the US.

The USDA formed its dietary guidelines in 1916 with the assistance of the American Dietetic lobby group. The old USDA Food Pyramid had been brought to us by a religious group based on one man's sexual obsessions and the hallucinations of a woman who had seizures after a fall. Whether we like it or not, government laws and regulations are often set by lobbyists of special interest groups.

John Kellogg never marched in protest against meat nor destroyed someone else's property. He focused on becoming competent and built long-lasting businesses and organizations to fulfill his religious fervor of a meatless world.

There are a couple of lessons to learn from this story. First, activism or evangelism is most successful when we grow personally. Second, the urge to save humanity can have disastrous consequences.

But you have to give Kellogg credit. He did achieve his goal of reducing the libido of American men. A chronic decline in testosterone in young men is one result of his actions.[29] Kellogg's inner stories led to massive changes in the health of the US population.

Activism often leads to painful unintended consequences

---

29   https://www.sciencedaily.com/releases/2018/04/180419100119.htm.

when it is backed by pseudo-science. Whether it is the devastating results of the Great Society on black families or the SDA's influence on our health, zealotry without real science hurts all.

Next Steps

Want to reframe your stories? Go to rebootmystories.com and learn helpful tips on creating a new world to live in.

PART VI
ADVANCED GROWTH SEEKING INTELLIGENCE PROGRAMS

Harland had successfully operated a motel with an attached restaurant in Asheville, North Carolina, during the 1940s. During World War II travel was limited due to gas rationing, and the motel and restaurant failed.

Harland tried again by building a restaurant in Corbin, Kentucky, that became popular with travelers on their way to Florida. But when Interstate 75 was completed in the 1950s—bypassing the town—Harland was forced to close the restaurant.

In 1952 at sixty-five years of age and living on his $105 a month Social Security benefits check Harland once again embarked on another career when most people would have retired. He began traveling across the country, cooking along the way, determined to franchise a fried chicken recipe he had developed. Many of the restaurant owners he met laughed at his signature starched white shirt, black tie, and white jacket and pants.

Pete Harman was a friend of Harland's and operated one of the largest restaurants in Salt Lake City. Harland persuaded Harman to allow him to sell his chicken in his Do Drop Inn restaurant. It was a success, increasing sales by 75 percent. Soon several more restaurant owners signed franchise agreements with Harland, for the princely franchise fee of four cents per chicken.

It was during this early franchise period that Harland met Dave Thomas. Thomas was a cook at the time. Thomas developed the classic wobbly red-and-white-striped chicken bucket for Harland that became the classic sign outside of each fried chicken restaurant. Thomas also streamlined the method of food-to-customer delivery by creating the "snake" line still used in many restaurants today.

Thomas took over eight failing restaurants and was so successful he was able to sell the restaurants and opened his own chain of hamburger restaurants, named after his daughter Melinda Lou "Wendy" Thomas.

Harland was Colonel Sanders who stepped outside his comfort zone into the unknown and developed a huge business.

By 1964 there were over six hundred franchised Kentucky Fried Chicken locations in the U.S., Canada, Mexico, England, and Jamaica. At age seventy-three, Harland sold most of Kentucky Fried Chicken to John Y. Brown and Jack Massey for $2 million.[30]

Sanders pushed into the chaos of the unknown when most people drop into retirement.

This growth model is what we will discuss next.

---

30   . From TheBalanceSMB.com.

40

THE CHAOS/ ORDER CONUNDRUM

I'VE USED THE word *triggers* liberally throughout this book without really delving much into its current cultural renaissance. College campuses are filled with trigger warnings and safe spaces for those wishing to avoid being triggered. Safe spaces are areas where students are protected from hearing about ideas contrary to their own beliefs.

Are safe spaces a good idea? Do we need to be protected from ideas that are different from our own?

As I mentioned at the beginning, we are creators that seek to bring order to chaos. Why? Our brain wants to find patterns, so it can reduce its workload. This is the principle of conservation of energy. However, the second law of thermodynamics (or law of entropy) states that in its natural state any system will degenerate into chaos.

In other words, the universe is always descending into disorder and chaos and our brain has to constantly work to make order out of the mess. The biblical story of creation is just that, intelligence begetting order out of chaos.

Our brain prompts us to get "control" over our life. So we create habits and routines because there is a sense of comfort in a state of order.

At one end of the order-chaos spectrum are extreme OCD types who are driven to control every detail of their lives—even down to the time for their bowel movements—so that things are as predictable as possible. Most people are not this extreme, but they still create lives that are deeply patterned so that they never feel uncomfortable or have to engage in uncharted waters. They get up at the same time every day; take the same route on their way to their job every day. They do the same tasks and interact with the same people. There is little joy in their existence and they often feel oppressed by the sameness of their routines but dare not change. Structure provides a sense of safety for their deep fears about the unknown. This is what the "safe spaces" fad is about.

The problem with too much order is that our lives become tyrannical. Too much structure takes away all our choices and freedom. That is why we feel oppressed by routine. If you have ever been driving to work and thinking, "Life doesn't have to be this way," you are reacting to the tyranny of order.

Civilizations create governments with lots of rules and regulations in order to make its people feel safe. In the end, the crushing weight of rules oppresses the same people with the tyranny of structure. This cycle is why governments are periodically overthrown. Nothing around us is staying static. It's constantly changing, descending into chaos, as are we—despite the illusion that we aren't. If you've ever worked to get your body in shape and then taken a few weeks off from diet and exercise regimes, you know how fast your body descends into disorder.

At the other end of the spectrum are people who seem to live in total chaos. Their lives are filled with lots of drama and turmoil. They are constantly seeking to get a new "high." The high of a chaotic life can be quite exhilarating. Our body releases lots of dopamine. However, it can also be quite deadly. When people have a Me story that creates large problems and is unresolved, they often fall into chaos as an escape from the responsibility of dealing with those issues. We examined some of them in the section on drama queens in Chapter 17.

Rather than grow personally some choose a story of blame and hopelessness and over time they medicate themselves with alcohol, drugs, food, or some other addictive behavior to numb the pain. In this manner, they can play the victim of their addictions and thus remaining powerless. These types of people seek out others who will enable their chaotic lives by reinforcing their identity as victims as we saw in Chapter 16.

If we have any kind of addictive behavior, there is most certainly part of our life that appears scary (chaotic). Our brain tries to avoid that with the "order" of the addiction. There is a comfort to doing the same things day after day even if that behavior is ultimately destructive.

But there is a more harmonic way to balance our life between order and chaos.

Think of chaos as that area of your life that is the unknown, things that you have not experienced. What makes you uncomfortable?

Your brain wants order to feel safe, while your heart wants adventure to feel alive.

Keep one foot in the order side to feel safe, and at the same time push yourself into situations that are new, uncomfortable, and force you to grow.

From an early age, I've always rebelled against order. My first memory is a second-grade coloring class. The teacher instructed us to color between the lines and in a parallel motion. I decided I was not going to comply. I wisely chose a yellow crayon so the teacher could not tell. I colored outside the lines in a zigzag manner. Unfortunately, there was a piece of a lead pencil embedded into the tip of the crayon, and I got caught!

Later in my life, I chose chaos over order when I decided to leave my parents and go off into the unknown as a teen. As an adult, even though I worked at the same company for nearly forty years, I spent my time trying to disrupt the status quo every chance I could. I used the order and security of my job to explore entrepreneurship. In my spare time, I built an Amway business, bought and renovated over twenty housing units, built websites and a SaaS business, ran for and served in political office, and much more. I explored the unknown while still keeping one foot in a safe zone. Let's just say I took risks after performing a safety assessment.

The next few chapters explore ways to take some risks.

41

THE RISK/SAFETY ASSESSMENT

ANOTHER WAY OF thinking about order and chaos is to use the terms safety and risk to examine our stories. Taking risks is a creative process where we explore the unknown. In successful risk taking, we have to ignore what others think as well as our own doubts. There are four primary kinds of risks: educational, financial, health, and social.

Two hundred years ago people had to risk their lives or their financial resources to put food on the table. In modern Western society, there is little risk of starving or being homeless thanks to the welfare state. (Those who choose to live on the street usually suffer from mental illness or addiction.)

Instead, almost all risk has been transferred to social status risk.

You risk your social status any time you engage with another person. To improve your social status you may take a financial risk by buying a bigger house than you can afford. The CEO of a giant corporation may risk their company's financials because they are afraid to take a social stand (e.g., having the "correct" social justice viewpoint in their TV ads ruined Gillette earnings causing P&G to take an $8B write-off).

People risk their lives trying to get the perfect selfie for their Instagram or Pinterest page so that they can get the dopamine rush of more likes. Companies like Facebook and Twitter are extremely effective at exploiting this weakness. The manipulation by these tech giants actually increases suffering for users and fits into my interpretation of evil behavior.

The chaos-order and risk-safety paradigms are like a neural network that forces itself to scour all the data available in its purview to learn new things and constantly upgrade its software algorithm. As the network gains more information, it increases its accuracy in controlling whatever it is in command of.

We must be able to understand the duality of risk and safety and embrace both simultaneously. We must understand when we are stuck in order and safety versus when we are overwhelmed in chaos and risk. The idea of duality is a strong theme in our existence. We have explored this idea in several different areas.

One way to explore this dynamic is by exploring social status risks. Taking social status risks is both the safest and provides the greatest lever for growth of all the risks. For many though this is the scariest risk to take. We often freeze or run from social status risks.

The following sections help you to explore taking risks and probe the unknown where you can expand your character and provide opportunities to craft exciting new stories.

42

SOCIAL RISK TAKING

SOCIAL STATUS RISK taking is the dominant perceived hazard in our current world. These encounters vary from the very intimate to the non-personal risks. I say it's a perceived hazard because social risk usually does not cause us to starve or freeze to death. Yet, people would often rather risk their lives literally rather than speak to a crowd, for example.

Some limits are real. Some limits are imagined. You won't know the difference until you attempt to push through them.

As mentioned above, living in close quarters with another person exposes us to social status risk quite a bit. This is especially true with the opposite sex. The yin-yang symbol represents male and female and order and chaos dichotomy for a reason. We all feel more comfortable with same-sex interactions because it represents more order to our brains.

When we first meet someone we often put on a mask to hide our real self. There is a huge social status risk in revealing our true selves, especially if we are sexually interested in the other person.

Remember sex is one of our evolutionally prime directives on Maslow's Pyramid.

In a close quarter relationship, over time, we will lapse in unmasking our true self because the other person will trigger us. What happens is our Me stories are exposed. All close quarter relationships either end with lots of blame, victim playing, and pain or with personal growth.

Some people try to avoid the potential pain by instead having one-night stands, but even these take a toll on our personal emotional health. Having to constantly hide our true self is stressful. These types of sexual encounters often involve manipulating another's emotions. You can probably guess that I view manipulating other people to get something we want as an evil endeavor.

Maybe the ultimate way to expose even more of our Me stories in a relationship is to live in close quarters with someone 24/7 on a boat or an RV where you cannot get away! I've lived this way for three years now, and it is very revealing what triggers come up. Sometimes issues that I thought I resolved years ago rear their ugly head again.

A more expansive social risk is having children. Even though they are not strangers in the normal sense, children expose us to a new chaos. Children are often brutally honest and can expose our Me stories with questions. Our Me stories can also be exposed when we find ourselves treating our children exactly as our parents dealt with us. And the more children you have, the more you are exposed to new triggers. Children change much more than adults do over a similar time period, so we are introduced to new people at each stage of their growth. I grew up with seven siblings, and we triggered our parents a lot. I seem to remember that at every family meal either my mom would turn beet red when one of us asked an inappropriate question or my dad got angry when one of us misbehaved.

Speaking in front of crowds is another way to expose ourselves to social risk. I've mentioned how the Amway program used to get me to be comfortable speaking one on one to someone all the way to being excited talking to five thousand plus people. Toastmasters is an organization that I once belonged to that can give you a similar experience.

Another way to expose yourself to chaos is to hang around people who are not like you. Immersing yourself with other races or cultures can push your comfort zone. It's not the color of someone's skin that makes us fear him or her, it's our own tribal stories about the unknown tribe that creates the fear. And if we are not afraid of them, are we judging them as inferior or superior to us?

When we spend time trying to understand others, we find that they have about 98 percent of the same fears and desires as us. There are universal stories that unite us. What interferes with our understanding of others is the stories we tell ourselves to protect our own Me story.

Another social risk is to voice a contrarian viewpoint in a social setting. Being attacked for having an unpopular position is the current day equivalent of being hunted by wolves on social media. We get triggered a lot. The same adrenaline is released. Having the confidence to defend our position exposes us to lots of social risks that may hurt us emotionally and financially as well.

People often act like sheep when it comes to contrarian viewpoints. They watch TV shows and read news stories that are aligned only with their point of view. All their social interactions are with like-minded people to avoid getting triggered. Think about who you hang out with. Do they all share your views?

Always be willing to listen to and watch other points of view. This is a sign of maturity. Being able to understand what is triggering you and stand on your own is a sign of considerable personal growth.

43

EDUCATIONAL RISK TAKING

EDUCATION CAN ALSO be risky. Going to college or vocational school represents a risk-taking venture for personal growth.

The key to doing this correctly is to not attend a school simply for the idea of getting credentials. Getting credentialed is a social status game not a personal growth play.

People often wrongly suggest that you should do what you love. As a result, people choose courses they like and agree with rather than courses that challenge their thinking and make them work. The more you have to work at learning a new subject, the more you grow and build your skills. The discipline needed to undertake a difficult course is also a valuable competency to acquire.

There are four criteria that are useful to determine whether you should pursue educational courses:

- Do you have some natural skills or talents to learn this?
- Is there a demand for it in the marketplace? Will someone pay you for this?
- Does the world need this?

- Do you enjoy this, or can you learn to enjoy it?

College is not the only place to take educational risks. Trade schools can give us proficiency in practical skills that are the basis for a functioning society. Keeping the electricity flowing, the plumbing working, and heat on are at the core of keeping society running.

The Internet provides plenty of opportunities to explore new ideas. The Internet allows us the ability to find someone who has actually accomplished something we wish to achieve. Contrast this with a professor who knows the theory but has no real-world experience.

Once I found successful people, I learned the best type of education comes from someone who has done what we want to do. I have found that traditional college courses were not as important to my success as what I learned from successful people. Successful people solve real-world problems with action. They don't espouse theories. Sam is someone I learned from who had accomplished a tremendous amount. Successful people are more accessible than ever, and crafting a plan to find them and seek out their practice knowledge can accelerate your path to success.

At some point in your life, when finances no longer play into your decisions about what to do, learning for the sake of learning is also a great way to expand yourself. You have the freedom to explore topics just for the sheer joy of learning.

44

PHYSICAL RISK TAKING

Physical risks also spur personal growth. Learning a new sport or to play a new musical instrument can challenge us (though what holds us back is often social risk—the fear of being ridiculed).

I learned to mountain bike in my fifties. I hadn't ridden a bike since I was twelve and certainly never a mountain bike or even a BMX. Going to mountain bike parks or riding single track trails with my initial low skill levels made for lots of embarrassing falls. I would often have to walk up or down steep, technical parts of the trails in front of ripped twenty-something's making it look easy.

Even now I am not an expert, but I became proficient enough that my wife and I were able to ride down the famous Whole Enchilada trail in Moab, Utah. The ride starts above twelve thousand feet and takes you along the edge of the Colorado River gorge where a small slip can deposit you several thousand feet down. To say the ride was thrilling would be an understatement! I went over my handlebars and landed on my head once, and every time I looked at the edge of the cliffs I would shake.

Going on an epic adventure often can help us get in tune with some of our Me stories if we're alone. Hiking the Appalachian or Pacific Coast Trails is an example of such an adventure. Most of the growth is overcoming our fear of being alone or away from the safety of civilization.

We took our RV on a ten-thousand-mile trip through Canada and up to Alaska. There were days we went without cell phone service, and it often was hundreds of miles between towns. We had a bear graze twenty feet outside our RV for several hours in a remote camping area of British Columbia. We were chased by a moose while biking in the wilderness of Wrangell-St Elias National Park. We saw countless wildlife, awesome mountain ranges and glaciers. We took a one-thousand mile side-trip on a dirt road, with no cell service and only one town, to the Arctic Ocean to boot.

Many people dream of taking adventures but fail to launch. They make excuses about time or money. However, often the thing really holding them back is fear of the unknown.

When we decided to sell our beautiful home and all its contents to live full time in an RV, we too had a lot of fear. Thoughts of not having a home base, being far from children, not knowing if the two of us could live in such a small space without killing each other played havoc on our minds.

Sometimes that fear created a story that we were crazy or insane. The key to getting over those stories is to prepare as well as you can. Luckily, we live in a time when it is easy to gain knowledge from other people's experiences. We joined several groups on Facebook and RV forums that allowed us to ask questions of others who lived the lifestyle we aspired to. We could see the good as well as the pitfalls in advance.

So plan your adventure, learn as much as you can beforehand, and then trust that you are capable to complete the journey.

45

FINANCIAL RISK TAKING

GOING INTO BUSINESS for yourself can expose you to financial risk as well as social risk. The gig economy lets us test out doing our own thing with little risk. Going all-in with a large investment and working full time on an entrepreneurial venture can be very thrilling and very rewarding.

When I opened an Amway business, I was exposed to the idea of taking a financial risk. I expanded my entrepreneurial ventures by investing in rental houses. I eventually accumulated over twenty houses. The houses were generally in poor condition, and I couldn't afford to hire expensive contractors to upgrade the houses. So I learned many skills: electrical, plumbing, heating, roofing, dry walling, and painting. I wish I had YouTube back then. It would have saved me thousands of dollars because I made many mistakes while learning these new skills.

I took more financial risks when I started a software as a service (SaaS) business. I founded *SherlockDocs.com,* a writing tool for Private Investigators. It was my first exposure to young entrepreneurs like Dane Maxwell and Sam Ovens. The most important part of that experience was learning how many tools were available for entrepreneurs to grow a business idea. I learned how to find competent and inexpensive contract employees, how to launch and market my services, and how to find the right people to connect with. There seems to be a software tool that solves every problem.

One of the benefits of the current explosion of technology is that we can reduce our risks with the knowledge that is out on the Internet. There is a blog or website or video that can educate us on just about any topic. There are websites like Upwork.com where you can sell your skills to the entire world without having to invest in your own website and marketing. There are young, Internet-savvy people who can help us navigate both cyberspace and business.

My friend Sam Ovens, who I mentioned at the beginning of this book, runs such a business at Consulting.com. He teaches people with a skill how to market that skill and become highly paid consultants.

Stepping into the chaos of financial risk taking is another lever you can use to build your talent stack. Not only will you learn about working with business finances, but you may also learn old school skills like electrical and plumbing as well as new school skills like HTML coding and building marketing funnels.

46

RISK TAKING PIVOT POINTS

---

*"People are open-minded about new things - as
long as they are exactly like the old ones."*

—Charles Kettering

ONE OF THE easiest ways to step into the unknown is when we are
going through a transition in life. A transition point is where we
are already letting go of old relationships or jobs or homes. Here
are some examples[31] of transition points:

- When moving geographically from one place to another.

- When entering or leaving a relationship.

- When an economic change occurs in our life from how
  we earn our living to a monetary loss or gain.

- When we have chosen or been forced into taking on new
  responsibilities like being a parent or caregiver or a boss.

- After tragedies or illnesses have altered our priorities.

I took advantage of the sudden change in my employment

---

31   . From *Story Theater Method* by Doug Stevenson.

status to sell everything, buy an RV, and travel North America for three years with my wife and dog. The sudden loss of a job had me wandering around my house aimlessly for a few months. Today, I move to a unique location every couple of weeks and explore the unknown. The sense of adventure and enjoyment I get by exploring new places and being immersed in nature has been incredible.

Experiencing the unknown makes our heart pump stronger and release our endorphins. However, having a life that is all chaos causes stress and releases lots of cortisol and adrenaline. The results of constant stress are high blood pressure, low energy, and loss of joy in our lives.

Living all on one side or the other of the order-chaos spectrum is not very healthy. We fight the tyranny of order and boredom of routine on one edge. On the other, we are stressed by chaos and unknown unknowns where our amygdala controls the stories we create. Living on the boundary between chaos and order can give us a more optimal life. We have a certain level of order and choose when and where to explore unknown territory.

Like a neural network, expanding our risk taking and venturing into new areas in one area builds our confidence and skills in other areas. Investing and learning about marketing helped me to sell my ideas at my job much better. Being able to take risks on a mountain bike helped me to see that taking financial risks was not that dangerous. Knowing that I could fix things—a skill and mindset I developed from owning rental houses—allowed me to not worry about my RV breaking down in the wilderness.

Scott Adams writes about the idea of building "talent stacks." When you push yourself into chaos in any of these areas—physical, financial, knowledge or social—you are automatically building a talent stack. The primary building block of any talent stack is self-confidence. You gain confidence by an ever-expanding list of accomplishments that you can access to craft new stories.

One of the challenges in setting large goals is that we cannot see a path to the goal. There is a large gap between where we are and where we want to go. The key to jumping the gap is to place many stepping-stones along the way. Some of these stones may not seem like direct paths, but they build your talent stack and give you the ability to create a self-confidence story. Take the skill of public speaking, for example. Your goal may be to build a not-for-profit organization or a web design company and think there is no need to learn public speaking. But our skills and self-confidence bleed over into other areas of our life. Learning to speak in public gives you the confidence to get on the phone with a large donor for your non-profit or sell a big contract for your web design company.

What keeps you from acting in areas where you are uncomfortable?

The stories you are telling yourself.

Push yourself into the realm of the uncomfortable and watch how you grow and find enjoyment in life.

Next Steps

Ready to take on a new adventure and explore the world? Go to rebootmystories.com for more information that can open your eyes to the possibilities the world offers.

PART VII
A NEW ALGORITHM

"Change is invigorating! If you don't accept new challenges you become complacent and lazy. Your life atrophies!"

—Calvin

47

THE GREAT STORY

WHAT IF THERE was a computer program that would guarantee you would have the greatest satisfaction from your life?

Well, there is such a thing and it's already preprogrammed into our psyche. We just need to know how to access it.

One of the most common storylines we enjoy in movies or books is the hero's journey. This is where a person goes on an adventure, encounters dark forces, and has a setback. They appear to be headed in the wrong direction, but then they encounter a guide who imparts wisdom on him or her. Then in a moment of crisis, they win a victory. The hero is transformed and comes home forever changed.

What if you could be the hero or heroine in your story? In first discussing stories I noted that we often like to see ourselves as the hero in our stories. The hero's journey story was recognized by author Joseph Campbell as a universal archetype. In other words, we all identify with this story on a very deep level and seek to live it out in our lives.

We so love this storyline that people who create movies or

write books depicting the hero's journey get very wealthy. Walt Disney's films from *Pinocchio* to *The Lion King* are all the same story retold. The reason we love this story so much is that we aspire to be such a hero. It's our built-in life's mission. It is the higher purpose we all want to have.

Being a hero doesn't mean we have to save someone from the dragon's lair. The definition of hero is *"a person who is admired or idealized for courage, outstanding achievements, or noble qualities."*

Here are the steps of the hero's journey:

1. A flawed protagonist enters the scene.
2. The protagonist is seeking something but not quite sure what.
3. The protagonist encounters a big problem.
4. There is a dark night of the soul where everything looks bleak and hopeless.
5. The protagonist encounters a guide that sheds some wisdom about the protagonist's character hidden to him or her ("the force is within you").
6. The protagonist undergoes a personal transformation.
7. The protagonist succeeds and becomes a hero.

Watch for this in movies and books. Then see how you can apply the concept to your life.

One of the keys to this kind of story is how we frame our purpose and actions. For example, being a parent requires lots of courage, and to do it well requires noble qualities and service to others (our spouse and children). When we see ourselves as serving others in whatever purpose we choose, then we have the elements needed for the hero storyline.

The other key to this story is to understand that personal transformation comes while under duress. Finding dark forces to overcome is the easiest part of this storyline. We all encounter "dark forces." For example, children act in ways that draw a reaction from their parents continuously. Our amygdala triggers us to react defensively. This conflict often causes parents to inflict physical or emotional trauma on their children. Overcoming this dark force (or tribal training) can be a great personal transformation.

Someone who reviewed this manuscript early on thought the opening story of the protagonist was dark. Actually, our darkest hours often provide the biggest opportunity for transformation. The person who reviewed the manuscript was in a dark place at the time. When we are at that point we have to choose what story we want to cling to. Not all journeys result in victory. Sometimes stories end in tragedy.

~

My dark night came after traveling to Russia to adopt a sibling group ages six to nine (three girls and a boy). As I noted, we had become experts at adopting children. A few years after our first three were out of diapers, we started exploring the idea of adopting sibling groups. Already in our forties, we didn't want to wait too long to have the large family we dreamed of. When we saw a brochure depicting a group of four siblings being offered separately we decided to save them from the possibility of losing each other.

We bought a fifteen-passenger van and found a new home. Right next door was a family that had adopted eighteen children and one was Russian! It seemed like the stars were aligned for this adventure.

We flew to Moscow, stayed with a host family for a couple of days, and then traveled overnight five hundred miles north of Moscow to an orphanage. After finalizing the adoption in court and becoming the legal parents of the four children, the orphanage director decided that it was an appropriate time to tell us the truth. He filled us with horror stories about life in the orphanage and the misbehavior of the oldest girl who had been sexually assaulted. They would often put her in a straitjacket. He informed us that the children likely suffered from fetal alcohol syndrome. I felt the pain these children must have endured and was excited to bring them to a new environment.

However, my ex had a different reaction. From that point until we left Russia, she cried uncontrollably. When we returned to Moscow to wait for the approval of visas for the children, a conflict developed between my ex and the host family in Moscow over the treatment of the boy, and we had to move to a hostel. In the one-room accommodation, the children misbehaved while my ex lay in bed in a fetal position crying. I was torn between comforting my ex-wife and maintaining control of the children. We were about a mile from the nearest food source, and I walked back and forth through strange neighborhoods three times a day to buy meals at the McDonald's. Visions of getting mugged in the unfamiliar streets filled my mind. Those weren't happy meals.

We returned to the US and I went back to work while my ex stayed home with the new siblings as well as our other three children. I would come home every day and rock the four Russian children. They were terrified of their new environment and my ex was not engaging with them. There was no joy at home. I suggested my ex get counseling. Six months passed then one day my ex came back from the counselor and gave me an ultimatum. I had to choose her and our first three or the four Russian children.

There was no discussion in advance or after. I felt numb from shock. I felt castrated.

My ex contacted the adoption agency that had coordinated the adoption and started to arrange for a new family for the four Russian children. During this period I had to travel away for a few days for business. To assist my ex, I contacted the large family next door to our new home to have them babysit the children for a couple of days.

As I returned from my trip and attempted to pick up the children, we saw a van leave the neighbor's house and rapidly drive by our new home. As I watched the van I saw the Russian children's faces glued to the windows staring at me. I had called only minutes previously to tell them we were coming. It appeared to be a kidnapping! We contacted the police who questioned the older children in the neighboring home. The police told us a court order had given custody of our four Russian children to the neighbor!

This was untenable to my ex, so we sued all the way to the West Virginia Supreme Court and won back controlling custody. The adoption agency agreed to pick up the children and relocated them to a family in Texas. But the nightmare was not over.

The family next door went on a media campaign to slander us. Our name appeared in the papers and on TV as alleged child abusers. My ex could not take the attention and left our home in the middle of the night with our first three children and went to her parent's home in Illinois. She never returned to West Virginia.

I ended up finding a new position available in my company in New York, and my ex joined me after several months. But our relationship was over. I spent the next few years in counseling and taking anti-depressants. One day while in a group therapy session I had an aha moment. I realized how I had played the victim. I decided I would take control of my life from that point on. A few weeks later I filed for divorce.

My dark night lasted about six years. In my case, I clung to old stories in the hope that life would return to the pre-Russian times. I acted like a eunuch believing submissiveness would win her approval. But sometimes a tragedy happens, and no one is the same. Sometimes it is best to accept the new reality and move on with life.

When going through a dark period in life, it is tempting to see it as a threat or react with anger. Depression is anger turned inward. The group therapy session helped me to see the reality of what I was experiencing. It would be easy to accept that I had been a victim in this whole saga. I lived that victim story for six years after the ultimatum.

Often when we have problems we seek outside guidance—a guru, doctor, counselor—to help us. I've done this for years. What I discovered was that the best guide is our internal voice. Learning to quiet the noise of our mind can reveal much-hidden wisdom. There's an old axiom, "When the student is ready, the teacher will appear." The teacher is there to remind us of what we already know. As Luke Skywalker learned, the force is indeed within us.

Although the therapists did not help me in any way, the group therapy session helped me. Not because of what was said to me. A moment of awareness from observing reality allowed me to comprehend that the force was within me. I had control and was not going to play the victim any longer. My freedom came by realizing I had the solution inside me and did not need a prescription. I had transformed my story and my life.

❧

I hope you can see how it is possible to take what many consider a normal life experience—raising children—and turn it into a hero's journey. We can frame our stories to be a hero at our job, in a volunteer activity, or in whatever purpose we chose. But there has to be stress. The challenges make us grow. The hormesis process for our minds and bodies to get stronger exists universally. Plus, without the dark night, our story is just not that interesting.

Suppose you are a manager of a small restaurant. In the beginning, you are only interested in this business as a way to make money. You often get triggered by your employees' poor work habits and government red tape. Sometimes even the customers annoy you with their petty complaints. Your restaurant is not a happy place and business is poor. Your financials are in the red, and you get angry every time you talk with your accountant.

At some point you realize that unless something changes your business will go bankrupt. You start to get sick of failing and experience this dark night of the soul. You seek out wisdom and find this book. Using the Debugging Software you start to analyze the source of these triggers and the Me stories surrounding them. After multiple times working through the process, you ponder a childhood trauma one morning while showering and have an aha moment. In that moment you undergo a personal transformation. You start to empathize with customers and employees. You see that both groups have Me stories that are triggering their stories and attitudes.

With this transformation, you find purpose in treating your customers as people in need of attention and love. Sometimes a smile or a kind word will lift their spirits and make their day go better. You see yourself serving a noble purpose in providing food that nourishes their bodies and a kind word that nourishes their spirit. And you decide that rather than criticizing and lording over your employees, start mentoring them and guiding their personal growth.

Amazingly business gets better. Customers wait in line to get in. Your profit-and-loss statement turns black. You find that all the attention you have given to your customers and employees has come back to you in the form of an outpouring of love.

Can you envision undergoing a similar transformation in some other area of your life? Maybe you have an epiphany about another trigger that leads to a change in your attitude and transforms your marriage, parenting, workplace, church or something else.

You don't have to be perfect. In movies, the hero always has personal flaws and is never the perfect human. The hero always has dark periods of their journey and lots of missteps along the path. Even after the victory, the hero remains flawed. All that has changed is his or her mindset.

I noted earlier that it doesn't matter too much in the grand scheme of life what purpose we choose. It's important to choose a journey that forces us to grow personally, doesn't harm others, and where we can see ourselves as the hero.

And when that journey keeps us balanced between chaos and order our life will be better.

48

THE
GREAT TRANSFORMATION

---

*"Progress is impossible without change, and those who
cannot change their minds cannot change anything".*

—George Bernard Shaw

THE PROTAGONIST IN the story at the beginning of this book is
about to jump. He is wishing he had never been born. But suddenly, someone appears next to him and jumps into the river.
Instead of thinking of committing suicide our protagonist dives
into the raging river and rescues the other jumper.

While recovering from the shock of jumping in an ice-cold
river, our protagonist has a vision of what would have happened
if he had never been born. And even though our protagonist had
thought his life useless and unimportant, it turns out that his
impact on his town had been profound. Like a butterfly flapping
its wings can cause a storm around the world, his life decisions
have had a cascading effect on his whole town.

You see, his family's savings and loan bank had transformed

the town from a group of drifters living in squalid tenements into homeowners and business owners. He had created the predecessor to the suburbs.

A child was alive because our protagonist had alerted the pharmacist, who he had worked for as a teen, to an error in a prescription.

And the hearing he had lost came from saving his brother, Harry, from drowning. Harry went on to become a war hero, saving thousands of men in a battle.

Maybe you've guessed that the name of our protagonist is George Bailey from the movie *It's a Wonderful Life*. This movie, originally released in 1946, has been shown every Christmas Eve on NBC affiliated TV stations in the US for decades. Depending on the tribe you grew up in you may have seen this every Christmas or not at all.

If you examine the plotline based on what you have learned in this book, you can see that George changed his story from what he believed was an oppressive, worthless life into a wonderful life. His transformation came from rewriting his memories of his past. He saw himself as a hero instead of being trapped in a job he hated. He was no longer a victim of his situation but instead in control of his own destiny.

George was actually on a hero's journey all along but had never recognized it as such. He had been resentful and bitter about his life until the transformation took place. He didn't have to walk on hot coals or spend decades in psychoanalysis. And not a thing had changed in George's life except the story he told himself.

Note that George's self-absorbed thoughts on the bridge were interrupted when he chose to serve someone else in trouble.

George's savior in this hero's journey was an angel named Clarence who guided him through the dark night of his soul. An angel is a representation of our inner voice. So you see George had awakened himself with a simple thought experiment initiated by listening to his inner voice.

Transformation of our thoughts and stories can be very hard or it can happen in a flash. Many people will cling to their old stories and claim it is too hard or impossible to change.

Yet, the truth is that the barrier to change can come down to a few factors:

- Overcoming our fear of the unknown.
- Rewriting the meaning of our memories.
- Changing our acceptance of tribal norms.
- Being willing to be honest with ourselves.

I stated earlier how important pattern recognition was to our brains. Patterns help our brains deal with the world and make us feel safe.

✌

I hope you see a pattern in the last two sections of this book. In Part IV we discussed story bugs that send us down a bad path: hallucinations, toxic people, cults, depression, and despair. In Part V we covered creating new story patterns or ways to view the world.

We script, direct, and act in all kinds of unique dramas, comedies, fantasies, and love stories. We have spent countless years crafting our current stories and to a high degree enjoy them (at least subconsciously). They represent the truth of our inner intentions. We play this out in the theater of our minds.

If you didn't like your story, you would long ago have changed the script. Maybe you are content with your stories or only mildly dissatisfied. Our brain is an energy conservation machine so it's likely we just had not generated the activation energy to change our story yet. Since our brains resist change, we have to be deeply dissatisfied before we will make significant and permanent plot transitions to our stories.

Some people are lucky, and the transformation occurs without their conscious intervention (like near-death experiences). Most of us, however, will have to spend the time and take some conscious effort to work on our triggers and analyze our Me stories.

One of the main reasons I wrote this book is to help people recognize the patterns of their lives for what they are. Your stories produce results, and you have to accept the results these stories produce. If you find that you are now deeply dissatisfied with the results your life stories are producing, then you now have the tools to transform your stories.

The algorithms that run Google search, Facebook, and Twitter all depend on learning to create new user experiences. Likewise, we can create a new algorithm for how we author our lives.

Creating new stories involves the work of using the feedback loop to find new revelations based on the reality of real-world results in the process documented in this book. Anyone can improve their life skill at whatever endeavor they wish to pursue. It involves training your brain to use your frontal cortex rather than your amygdala to react to trigger events.

∽

With my engineering background, I used to think that only facts mattered. But I have found that stories rule humanity. It is the stories that control how we interpret the facts.

Here are the lessons I hope you were able to glean from this book:

- Our brain creates stories from memory patterns it has stored.

- Our stories and memories are infinitely malleable. We can write stories that give us exactly the life we want; limited only by physics.

- Our emotions are the servants in our stories not our master.

- We need a purpose that is meaningful not just expedient.

- We can create a system that incentivizes us by hacking our own dopamine.

- We need to be aware of our confirmation bias when evaluating results.

- Feedback loops will serve to exponentially increase our results.

- When interacting with others consider the possibility that they are suffering from their "Me" stories, which involve human craving to be loved and understood.

- Understand that we are all connected and how we treat others will reflect back on us. We are all responsible for the evil and good we put out in creating the world we see.

- Forgive others when we get triggered. Look at the trigger as solely our responsibility to fix.

- Our problems are all about us. Stop playing the victim.

I mentioned at the beginning that it's not about the journey; it's about the destination. So why am I suggesting you adopt a hero's journey? The point is not that you go through all the trials and tribulations on this journey. The point is that you see that your personal transformation is the destination. The moment you see how malleable your life is, where you see that triggers and emotions no longer control you, and you know you no longer need to seek attention by playing a victim, you will have arrived. That is total freedom.

I used "we" in the list of lessons above because this book is as much about my learning as it is a help for you. I found as a teaching assistant in grad school we only master information when we have to teach others. I am connected to you now that you have read my book. My hope is that we can reverse Dostoyevsky's declaration about our collective responsibility for evil and turn that into collective good.

Create a hero story, not a victim story. Create a gratitude story, not an envy story.

Change your story; change your life.

49

EXAMINING PIVOTAL
MOMENTS & TALENTS

*"It was the best of times, it was the worst of times, it
was the age of wisdom, it was the age of foolishness, it
was the epoch of belief, it was the epoch of incredulity,
it was the season of light, it was the season of darkness,
it was the spring of hope, it was the winter of despair."*

—Charles Dickens,
Tale of Two Cities

HAVE YOU EVER examined your life and looked at pivot points?
Are there times when you changed your story and your subsequent
life changed dramatically as a result?

I've mentioned a few examples of them throughout this book.

My encounter with Sam Ovens in his Master Mind event
pivoted me from being a retired homeowner and landlord into a
free-roaming RV'er.

In my decision to become a chemical engineer and go to

a co-op[32] college I turned my parents' difficulties with money into a steady paycheck that will last until my wife or I die, and I avoided the large, burdensome student debt load many college grads have today.

And the Russian adoption fiasco can rate high up (or more accurately, down) there with pivotal moments. My parents were there during the crisis. They supported me both emotionally and financially.

But probably the most pivotal moment with respect to my mindset came when my parents exposed me to Amway in my thirties. Every year I drove over 100,000 miles to sales meetings and conferences. Often I would drive all night after a sales meeting only to return home in time to go to my job. I had a fair number of encounters with police, wild animals, and waking up as my car was about to veer into a ditch. I lost many friends who shunned me. I was often mentally and physically exhausted and had to turn on a happy face every time I was with people. In many ways, it was a painful experience.

I cannot recommend multi-level businesses as a way to make money or achieve financial freedom. One of the big lies around this type of business is that once you build your network of distributers large enough, you will have passive income and can "retire". Actually, as your network grows, the workload increases. Close to a thousand people passed through my network. Only a few stuck with me so it was a battle to constantly add new faces. But for a decade I forced myself to enter into the unknown. Probing the unknown was what made the experience worth every minute.

At its heart, Amway is a personal sales business that forces you to encounter people one-on-one. As I pointed out earlier, being one-on-one with people exposes your Me stories. I spent

---

32 . Co-op colleges like Northeastern University offer the opportunity to alternate full time work semesters with full time college course semesters.

many evenings in the kitchen or living room of complete strangers trying to sell them on the possibility that they could achieve their dreams. Subconsciously I doubted whether I could have mine. As an introvert, I was always uncomfortable. My body would be sweaty, my mouth dry, and my heart pounding. As I pushed myself and succeeded (I have my name on the wall of fame at Amway headquarters), I had the opportunity to speak in front of large groups of people. It terrified me in the beginning, but I dealt with it. The action of building my business forced me to grow.

In addition to the personal growth, I had the opportunity to hear successful people speak of their journeys. I heard Zig Ziglar, Johnny Cash, Les Brown, President Ronald Reagan, and hundreds of others speak. These people introduced me to the ideas that revolutionized my thinking. I learned that:

- Learning is a lifelong endeavor.
- I control my own destiny.
- The opportunity and ability to make money by delivering something of value to others is everywhere.
- We live in the best of times.
- Life is a journey and the best part is really enjoying the journey not necessarily reaching the goals.
- It didn't matter what others thought of me.

The speakers even forced me to reflect on and ultimately change the course of my spiritual life.

The most important idea I took away from Amway was the importance of the environment and people we surround ourselves with. We become that to which we are consistently exposed.

For me, the Amway experience was both the best and toughest experience of my life. Have you had an experience that encompassed both misery and exhilaration? Examining what has happened in your past can show you that you too have changed stories throughout your life. Nothing was permanent, though at the time you may have believed that to be true.

The Amway experience was one part of a large talent stack that I have built in my life. Each of the little skills I learned contributed to my overall sense of confidence. Here's a partial list of my talent stack:

- Cooking
- Public speaking
- Sales
- Chemical Engineering (many subsets of skills)
- Statistics and data analysis (my most valuable talent)
- Creativity (My name is on a few US Patents)
- Driving and backing up forty-one-foot trailers
- Adoption
- Parenting
- Plumbing
- Electrical wiring
- Heating and ventilation
- Roofing
- Drywall and painting
- Problem diagnosis and troubleshooting
- Website design
- HTML coding
- Product launch
- Persuasion
- Google and Facebook advertising
- Infusionsoft (a contact management software)
- Automated online marketing funnels
- Product development

- Languages
- Biohacking
- Writing and publishing books

There are many more. You have developed multiple talents as well. Start a list of them. You most likely already have many talents that you don't even think of in this manner. Then build new ones to complement the old ones. One of the travesties of our time has been the specialization craze. Doctors are particularly vulnerable to this trend. They tend to ignore the whole body when treating their one specialty. Having a broad skill set will give you more confidence in your next endeavor, whatever that may be.

I hope this is inspirational to you and will motivate you to examine your pivotal moments and seek to grow by opening up your world to new experiences.

Best wishes on the adventure you now know you can write, direct and live!

Next Steps

Want to learn more about how you can be a hero in your life? Go to rebootmystories.com where I explore how you can be a hero.

50

DEBUGGING SOFTWARE QUICK SUMMARY

A. Clarification

1. Explain your trigger.
2. Who are you angry with?
3. Think back and write down. What is the story that you told yourself (and others) about this situation?
4. Is your story true? Are you 100 percent sure it is true? What real evidence do you have to prove it is true?
5. What feelings arose in you when you believe this story to be true?
6. What actions happened as a result of those feelings? What did you do?
7. Will the current story give you the results you want for yourself and others?

B. Introspection

    1. What is your Me story?

    2. What is the other side of your current story?

C. Transformation

    1. What is your ideal story?

    2. After examining all these viewpoints and possible stories—which one would you like to happen?

    3. What is the revelation, insight or lesson you've learned from this process?

D. Redirection

    1. This revelation is actually a new story. What feelings are you having about what you learned?

    2. What actions will you take based on these new feelings?

    3. If your old story resurfaces what will you do to break this roadblock?

E. Incentivization

    1. Build a system to reward yourself for small incremental victories with activities that give you a dopamine hit.

Acknowledgments

I've read hundreds of books on how to improve one's life, and I'm sure pieces of many of them are reflected in this book. More recently, work by Dr. Jordan Peterson (several of his twelve rules for life appear in the book), Perry Marshall (the idea of stories and, of course, 80/20), and Byron Katie and Garrett J. White (the process evolved from both their works) play heavily in my thoughts. Many thanks to all who have influenced my life.

Thanks to others who have influenced or inspired me:

Sam Ovens, for living the theme of this book.

Dane Maxwell, for demonstrating authenticity.

Robert Cormier, for teaching me no gain without pain.

Dexter Yager, for my real education, "Don't let anyone steal your dream."

Rolf Weberg, for your encouragement and kind words.

Josh Raab, for your insight in developing the major sections of the book and the flow.

Geoffrey Stone and Johanna Petronella Leigh for making sure the manuscript was clear.

Finally, I thank my wife, Jinna, for putting up with me while I wrote this.

BIO

The oldest of eight children, Paul was released from the shackles of a mental prison and went on to build a large talent stack: plumbing, electrical, real estate investing, entrepreneurship, chemical engineering and statistics to name a few. He has no credentials from an Ivy League school but he has developed a much greater skill than can be taught in a classroom: the ability to create the stories that drive his life.

Paul and his wife, Jinna, and their old dog are full-time adventurers. He has cycled up Pikes Peak, RV'd over most of Canada, Alaska, and the lower forty-eight. He's the father to many adopted children. He's worked on dozens of unique scientific discoveries and even has a few patents with his name on them.

Reboot distills decades of investigative work into how the mind works and how anyone can get the life they really want.